BUDDHISM

BERNARD FAURE

BUDDHISM

KONECKY & KONECKY

Translated by Sean Konecky.

The translator would like to thank Regan Konecky
for invaluable assistance and Tracy Davis. Her
knowledge of Buddhism and editorial skill
greatly improved my translation.

Konecky & Konecky
150 Fifth Ave.
New York, NY 10011

ISBN: 1-56852-188-X

Layout by Studio 31

Printed and bound in Italy

What is Buddhism? For some a religion, for others an atheistic philosophy, a means of obtaining salvation, an ethic, a view of the cosmos, a psychology, a political ideology. In the Buddhist parable of the blind man and the elephant, each of the blind men touched a part of the elephant and took the part for the whole. Then each tried to explain to the others what the animal was like.

Despite various interpretations, historians and commentators must agree on at least one point: Buddhism derives from the teachings of one man, Shakyamuni, the Buddha, although we will see that in the tradition of Mahayana Buddhism in which Shakyamuni is only one of the figures in the Buddhist pantheon even this point is disputed. A simpler definition is to identify Buddhism with the Three Jewels: the Buddha, the Dharma (Buddhist doctrine), and the Sangha (the community of believers). In Indo-Tibetan tantrism [?] there is a fourth Jewel: the guru or spiritual teacher. It is in these that the faithful place their trust as they recite at the moment of their conversion the formula of the Triple Refuge:

I take refuge in the Buddha.
I take refuge in the Dharma.
I take refuge in the Sangha.

In one form or another, Buddhism progressed across all of Asia: from India to China, Korea, and Japan, as well as to Tibet and Central Asia, moving from one oasis to another along the Silk Route. It spread to Iran, perhaps even Syria, and southeast through the Vietnam peninsula. It also traveled to Indonesia and Sulawesi. Recent archaeological finds have even discovered traces of its presence in the Maldives.

The story of Buddhism is that of almost half the human race over twenty-five centuries. So one should not be surprised if the story that follows contains lacunae here and there.

Page 2: *Two monks at Angkor.*

Opposite page: *Sixteenth century Tibetan painting.*

Following spread: *The Wheel of Life, representing the various states of being. Baoding Shan monastery, China.*

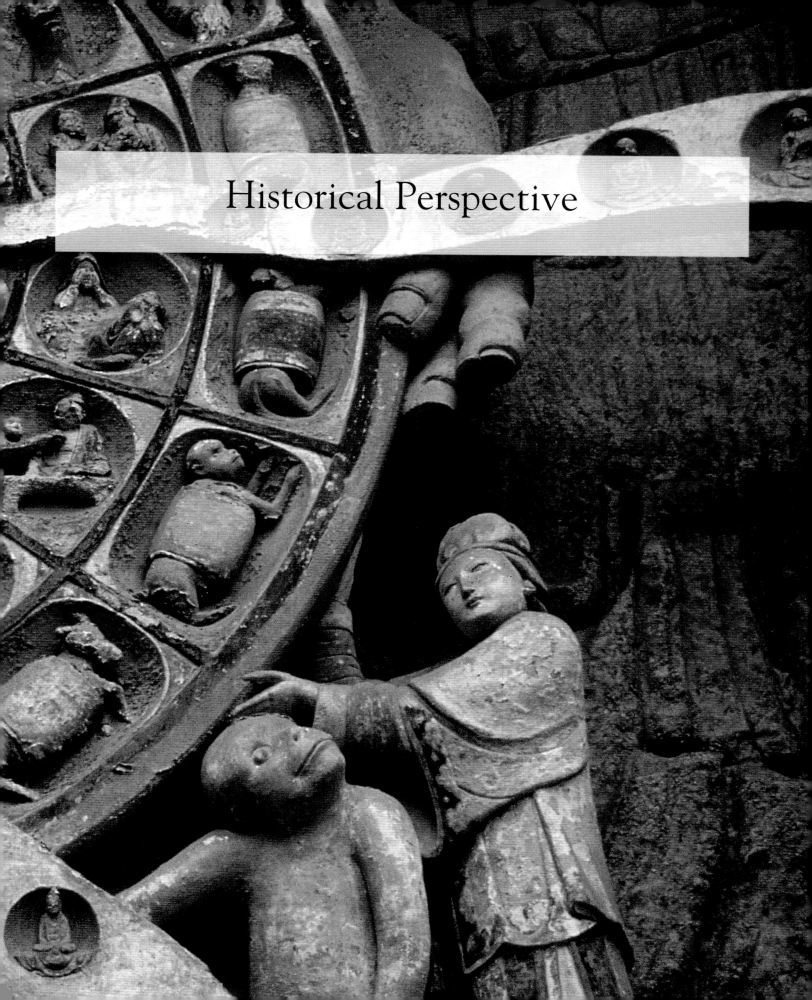

Historical Perspective

The Buddha and his Doctrine

Paul Mus has said of Buddhism, "India produced it and India explains it." Yet surely the Buddha, the supreme individual, cannot be explained only by his social context. The final lesson of Buddhist teaching — to attain deliverance — seems independent of all cultural contexts. But Buddhism itself is at once a social and a religious movement. The image of the Buddha, as it was transmitted throughout history, reflects the society that gave birth to it and was modified by those that came after.

What then is the original social and religious context? To simplify, let us say that the Indian world view encompassed both social and ideological elements in a hierarchical structure within which all elements find their proper place. At the center are the sovereign and the priest. Thus, the palace and the temple are but two facets of the same politico-religious power. In reality, the situation was much more complex.

The traditional thesis according to which the Buddha summarily rejected the two principal forms of authority is somewhat superficial. Certainly he argued against the Vedic or Brahmanic religion and its practice of ritual sacrifice. Moreover, the community that he founded appears to have been more egalitarian than the caste system of the surrounding society. But, like all monasticism, it did not remain egalitarian. According to tradition , the Buddha symbolically united within himself the two traditional forms of authority, the royal and the religious.

Classic Brahmanism transformed itself under the influence of certain social

Brahmanism or Vedism. Sacrificial religion founded on the Vedas (sacred scriptures) and the cult of Brahman (the ultimate principle behind all manifestation) led by brahmans (priests).

Scenes of the life of the Buddha. Sanchi, Bhopal, India. The aniconism of the stupa is balanced by anthropomorphic images on the peripheral bas-reliefs. This is a constant in Indian art: a central non-anthropomorphic image surrounded by divinities in human form.

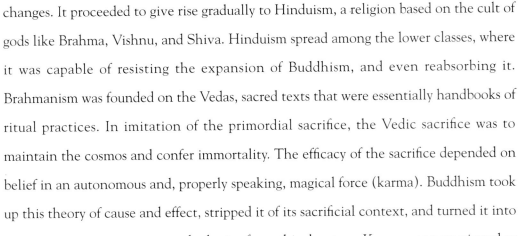

Brahma and Indra inviting the Buddha to preach. Bas-relief, Rome, Museum of Oriental Art. After attaining enlightenment under the Bodhi tree, the Buddha hesitated to teach the truth that he had just realized, thinking that humans were not ready to receive it. The intervention of two Hindu gods, Indra and Brahma, was required to persuade him to spread his message. This episode has caused commentators some embarrassment.

changes. It proceeded to give rise gradually to Hinduism, a religion based on the cult of gods like Brahma, Vishnu, and Shiva. Hinduism spread among the lower classes, where it was capable of resisting the expansion of Buddhism, and even reabsorbing it. Brahmanism was founded on the Vedas, sacred texts that were essentially handbooks of ritual practices. In imitation of the primordial sacrifice, the Vedic sacrifice was to maintain the cosmos and confer immortality. The efficacy of the sacrifice depended on belief in an autonomous and, properly speaking, magical force (karma). Buddhism took up this theory of cause and effect, stripped it of its sacrificial context, and turned it into the basis of an ethical system. Karma was now viewed as actions with moral consequences. In reaction to Vedic ritual, there arose an ascetic movement in Hinduism, Vedanta. Vedanta was founded upon the Upanishads, highly philosophical texts in which sacrifice is replaced by knowledge and understanding.

Important social changes around the fifth century B.C.E. produced the sudden appearance of ascetics who rejected all responsibilities to family and society. In particular, these men did not retain the fire sacrifices of Brahmanic ritual. They internalized the fire. They immolated themselves through ascetic practices. The Buddha was at first one of them. Another celebrated

Upanishads.
According to the Upanishads all reality is contained in Brahman, a pure, absolute, eternal essence, identical to *atman,* or Self, the immortal principle in humans. This divine spark, which makes the human being a

microcosm of the universe, has been covered by the veil of illusion *(maya)* has to bee reunited with its source, Brahman. To do this, the individual must break the chain of karma, the endless cycle of births and rebirths that makes up the illusory world

(samsara). liberation, *moksha,* is attained through ascetic practice and the transformation of consciousness.

ascetic was Mahavira, the founder of Jainism. He was also the son of one of the kings of northern India, who during a long period of meditation became the *jina*, the conqueror of the world.

Buddhism was founded on the same bases as Vedanta and Jainism. Like the asceticism of the Upanishads, it brought into question the idea of the Vedic sacrifice, but it also rejected the Vedic belief in *atman* (the supreme self). Like Jainism, Buddhism preached liberation from *samsara* (cyclic existence), but it insisted upon the unreality of the individual soul. In one sense Buddhism then was as much a continuation of Brahmanism as it was a reaction against it. The continuity is easily overlooked if one examines only the philosophical doctrine, but it becomes evident when practices and beliefs are considered. All these religious movements of ancient India were propelled by the actions of the ascetics who, by abandoning society and seeking out solitude, discovered an unprecedented individuality.

The cults of stupas and relics in Buddhism must also be seen in a historical context. The oldest Buddhist stupas were built on top of megalithic cemeteries, which suggests that the early Buddhists deliberately rooted their cults in the funerary practices of more ancient Indian

Statue of the Buddha from the Gupta period. Sanchi, Bhopal, India. The art of this period, in which physical features are typically Indian, put an end to the Gandhara period, which shows the influence of classical Greece. A rather sterile controversy continues over whether the origins of Buddhist figurative art are Greek or Indian.

At bottom: *Offerings to Mahavira.*

Jainism. Jainism is quite similar to Buddhism in a number of respects, although it is more radical in its asceticism. It is known primarily for its uncompromising ideal of non-violence *(ahimsa)*. Jains refuse to engage in any form of violence, whether secular (as in war) or sacred (as in ritual sacrifice).

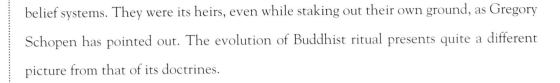

Buddha in meditation. Cave 17, Ajanta, India. In the course of a long period of meditation beneath the Bodhi tree in Bodhgaya, India, Shakyamuni realized the Four Noble Truths and attained enlightenment to be consecrated as the Buddha. Sitting meditation in the lotus position became the emblem of Buddhist practice.

Below: *Ascetics of Kakasama. Detail, Museum of Oriental Art, Rome.*

belief systems. They were its heirs, even while staking out their own ground, as Gregory Schopen has pointed out. The evolution of Buddhist ritual presents quite a different picture from that of its doctrines.

The Life of the Buddha

Many things have been said about the life of the Buddha. Historians have endeavored in vain to separate historical fact from fiction. In reality, we know nothing about the life of Shakyamuni. Historical reconstructions are based on dubious testimony that is just as pious and imaginative as the myths and legends they are intent on discrediting. What credit should we give to the tale of the death of Shakyamuni's mother seven days after his birth, when we know that this is exactly the fate of all the mothers of all the Buddhas? Or of the proposition that during his sheltered childhood the Buddha never had the slightest presentiment of disease, old age, and death? The truth of the Buddha is surely more accessible through his legend than through the historical facts. This legend, briefly, is as follows: Because of merit accumulated over the course of many past lives Shakyamuni was born as the prince and heir of a small kingdom in northern India and grew up amid princely pleasures and interests. During an

Ascetics. Paradoxically, some ascetics (the Jains in particular) came to exalt the individuality they realized through renunciation while others found it to be an encumbrance that had to be overcome either by merging with the cosmic Brahman (in Vedantism) or by denying its reality (in Buddhism).

excursion from his palace, he saw the conditions of a sick man, an old man, and a cadaver and became conscious of the emptiness of human existence. This experience led him to abandon his kingdom, his young wife, and his newborn son. He then embarked upon a solitary ascetic practice that was to last for six long years. There followed many different experiences and initiations, one of which was the temptation by Mara, the embodiment of confusion. After a time he attained liberation under the tree of awakening (the Bodhi tree). Having realized the truth, he gathered around himself a group of faithful disciples.

The first sermon, or turning of the Wheel of the Dharma, took place in the Deer Park at Sarnath (near Benares). Many other sermons followed over the course of a career that spanned forty years. His missionary work ended in a grove near Kushinagara. Like his birth, his death — or rather his entry into final nirvana (*parinirvana*) — and his cremation were marked by a series of miracles.

The story of early Buddhism is essentially that of a community of missionaries, believers, and pilgrims. It was the growing legend of the Buddha, rather than any codified doctrine, that fostered the vigor and life of early Buddhism. The new religion

Detail of the fresco of a thousand buddhas, Cave 2 Ajanta, India. The caves at Ajanta were dug out and painted over a long period starting in the second century B.C.E. and lasting until the seventh century C.E..

Below: *Prince Siddhartha (Shakyamuni) leaving his palace. Wall painting, Dambulla, Sri Lanka.*

Chronology. The dates for the Buddha are purely conventional, with no probable basis in fact: Ca. 566–486 B.C.E.

The great departure. When a Buddhist postulant leaves his family, he symbolically replays the Buddha's departure from his palace. In Cambodia, for example, the ordination ceremonies are an elaborate production during which the young man, mounted

on horseback like Shakyamuni, has to pass through a group of opponents playing the roles of Mara and his army, who try to prevent him from entering the monastery.

Standing Buddha. Bronze, from early seventh century, the end of the Gupta period in northern India.

Below: *Veneration of the Buddha, Museum of Oriental Art, Rome. In early representations the Buddha appears in a symbolic form. Here, the stupa, which contains his relics and was animated by them, serves as his architectural double.*

was organized around stupas, monuments that commemorated the events of the Buddha's extraordinary life. Four stupas were of particular importance: those associated with his birth, his awakening, his first sermon, and his death. These all became flourishing pilgrimage sites. The Buddha's followers had begun to recast his life in monumental form.

The activity of one of the early pilgrims and believers, Emperor Ashoka, would have a vast effect on the development of Buddhism. His pilgrimage to Lumbini, the Buddha's birthplace, is especially noteworthy, since we are able to pinpoint its exact location by the commemorative pillar he erected there. Without Ashoka's efforts, it is likely that Buddhism would have remained a minority religion like Jainism, which it resembles in several respects. According to legend, the emperor built eighty thousand stupas throughout India — and beyond, some even in China — to house the Buddha's relics. Ashoka's devotion to Buddhism came to be seen as a paradigm for the relationship of religion and the state throughout Asia.

Just as it is nearly impossible to separate the facts of the Buddha's life from the legends surrounding it, so it is to reconstitute the Buddha's Buddhism. We possess only textual reliquaries, and it is not even certain that they contain actual relics. In other words, the only Buddhism to which we can gain access is that of his followers, and his teaching was no doubt considerably modified in the process of transmission. The very idea of an initial teaching, preserved more or less intact beneath various later accumulations and remaining to be "rediscovered," ought to be viewed with caution. It

Cult of stupas.
In visiting these high places believers felt themselves to be reliving every episode of the glorious life of their teacher and could anchor their imaginations in particular places. The stupas were not simply commemorative monuments; they were principally reliquaries, containing the Buddha's corporeal remains (*sharira*) believed to have magical properties. Contact or proximity with them could increase the chance of happiness in this world and salvation in the next.

is reasonable to assert that Buddhist doctrine was invented by the Buddha's followers.

The Dharma

According to some Buddhist texts after the Buddha's *parinirvana*, the devotion of the faithful was to be channeled toward the two remaining Jewels: his Dharma, or doctrine, and his Sangha, the community of practitioners. According to another tradition, the Buddha had declared to his disciple Ananda: "After my death, each of you should be your own island, your own refuge. There is none other."

Early Buddhist doctrine, or Dharma (literally, "Law"), as it is usually presented, can be reduced to just a few significant concepts. According to the Theravada tradition, the Buddha refused to enter into metaphysical disputes and sought only to enunciate certain fundamental principles to serve as a practical guide for aspirants. Essentially these principles are contained in the Four Noble Truths: the truth of suffering, the truth of the origin of suffering, the truth of the end of suffering, and the Eightfold Path, which leads to the total extinction of suffering.

Ellora Cave, India. The apogee of Buddhist art in India can be found in the caves at Ellora and Ajanta.

At left: *Sarnath, where the Buddha is said to have delivered his first sermon. Today, only the ruins of monasteries built on the spot remain.*

The Four Meetings. Silk painting. From top to bottom: An old man, a sick man, a corpse, a monk.

The Four Noble Truths are based on two seemingly contradictory principles: There is no self (*atman*), and we are responsible for our actions (karma). Suffering derives from belief in a self that is illusory. In reality, only suffering exists, but there is no one who suffers. At the same time, action exists, but there is no one to act. Nirvana can be attained, but there is nobody to attain it; the path beckons, but there is no traveler. Personality is nothing more than a series of physical and mental phenomena, known as the five aggregates (form, sensation, perception, mental formation, and awareness). It has no more reality than the aggregates that compose it. This absence of self makes Buddhist morality somewhat problematic. If there is no self, then who is responsible and over whom does the law of karma rule? Without a transmigrating self, what fear is there of being reborn in undesirable circumstances?

The narrow interpretation of absence of self that Hinayana Buddhism preached was applied in Mahayana Buddhism to all dharmas (objective elements of the external world, not to be confused with Dharma, the Law). Whereas the first Buddhists gave some credence to the reality of external phenomena, the Buddhists of the Mahayana, or Great Vehicle, came to affirm the essential emptiness of all things. In good dialectical fashion, the emptiness of the argument for emptiness was also affirmed. This taste for emptiness should not be equated with nihilism. Paradoxically, it becomes, in practice, a reaffirmation of the world of the senses. In effect, although all negation involves a minimal affirmation (of the reality that is denied) and derives its force from that, there is no need to deny that which does not in itself have any reality.

Karma.
The law of karma entails transmigration from one existence to another and the individual's rebirth in one of the six destinies: that of the hell beings, the *pretas* (hungry ghosts), the animals, human beings, the *asuras* (titans), and the *devas* (celestial beings).

The Four Noble Truths.
The first truth is that suffering is the primary characteristic of all forms of existence, even the most seemingly pleasant ones. The second truth teaches that all suffering comes from desire, or craving, which leads to continuing rebirths in the world of *samsara*. This causality is defined in a more technical fashion as conditioned origination (Sanskrit: *pratitya-samutpada*). In other words all phenomena, physical or mental, are interdependent and

Buddhists found a way out of this seeming paradox with the notion of the Two Truths, one conventional, the other ultimate. That which is empty when seen from the point of view of the ultimate truth, conserves some reality from the conventional point of view. In practice, despite the teaching of the absence of self the majority of Buddhists accept the notion of an intermediate state of being, a sort of psychic distillation, which assures the connection from one rebirth to another. This disembodied but nonetheless gendered being wanders between the two worlds (the *bardo* of the Tibetans) until it is irresistibly drawn by its karma to the human or non-human womb in which it begins it next life. At the same time accepting the teachings of the Four Noble Truths does not prevent most Buddhists from aspiring to a better rebirth, and leaving the remote apotheosis of nirvana to monks and other serious aspirants.

Emaciated Buddha, Gandharan style. Lahore Museum, Pakistan. Having subjected himself to the harshest imaginable mortifications for over six years, Shakyamuni finally opted for the Middle Way, the path between asceticism and self-indulgence.

The Sangha

After attaining liberation, the Buddha undertook to show the path to others, thus becoming the founder of a religious community, the Sangha, comprising a monastic

without any independent nature. Even ignorance, desire, and hatred— the three poisons that contaminate existence and turn the wheel of *samsara* — are fundamentally without reality. The third truth teaches that the cessation of desire brings about the cessation of suffering, the supreme detachment that is nirvana. The fourth truth shows the Eightfold Path that the aspirant must follow to escape suffering: right view, right thought, right speech, right action, right livelihood, right effort, right mindfulness, and right meditation. The Eightfold Path is arranged under three headings: morality (*shila*), meditation (*samadhi*), and wisdom (*prajna*).

Monastery in Northern India. The first Buddhist monasteries grew up around stupas. Buddhism in these early days seems to have been essentially a cult of relics. In addition to religious seekers who dedicated themselves to meditation and their personal salvation, the laity as well as monks and nuns came to offer their devotion to the Buddha, hoping thereby to obtain a favorable rebirth.

order and a lay brotherhood. The monastic order was initially composed solely of monks, but eventually the Buddha resolved to open the community to women — not without warning that their presence would sow the seed of the Dharma's irreversible decline.

This initial tension heavily influenced the destiny of the monastic order and helped to keep nuns in a state of dependence. There was also tension between monks and laity, evident from the very beginnings of Buddhism in the division between the ideal of renunciation and that of active compassion. The ideal of compassion was to find its fullest expression in the Great Vehicle, the Mahayana. Whereas in early Buddhism the lay person whose virtues did not permit him or her to attain nirvana was clearly inferior to a member of the religious orders who strove for enlightenment, in Mahayana Buddhism the ideal represented by Vimalakirti, a lay person, supplanted that of the monks. In the *Vimalakirti-sutra*, Vimalakirti, who represents the compassion of the lay Bodhisattva, makes fun of the Buddha's disciples, who are seen as mournful saints overly attached to their illusions of purity.

Among the laity it is necessary to distinguish those whose fervor approached that of the clergy and the ordinary people who were content to accumulate, through their

Nirvana.
The distinction some have made between "karmic Buddhism" and "nirvanic Buddhism" is no more substantial than that between the laity and the religious orders, since many members of the latter were content to offer their devotion to the Three Jewels. To them, meditation was just one ritual among many others.

Vimalakirti-sutra.
The author of this treatise developed certain "heretical" ideas derived from Mahavira, said to be at the root of the Mahasamghika schism.

positive actions, the merits that assured them a favorable rebirth. They also hoped to reap some of the benefits in their present lives.

A similar distinction applies, in a sense, to the clergy. The first Buddhists were renunciants. In principle, these solitary individuals did not have fixed abodes. They lived by begging and wandered through India for the greater part of the year, returning to their communities only for the annual summer retreat. Others established themselves in villages and cities where there were monasteries and convents. A certain number of monks and nuns lived there permanently.

Urban monasteries soon flourished. The prosperity of Buddhism was due part to the generosity of Ashoka, who, as a pious and zealous sovereign, encouraged reforms. Under the deleterious influence of this material prosperity, religious practices weakened and became degraded. In contrast to their urban counterparts a minority of monks continued asceticism and meditation in the solitude of the forest. Their ideals of renunciation did not harmonize with the compromises needed in the larger monasteries. One cause of the schism that finally divided the community was the question of whether monks could possess money.

Some historians see in the advent of Mahayana

Monks. Wall painting from Sarcuq, eighth or ninth century, National Museum, New Delhi, India. The monastic code, essential to the smooth functioning of the community, is a symbol of unity. When different communities developed different codes, the result was a proliferation of different sects.

Monastic life.
The rhythm of life in Buddhist monasteries is governed by diverse rituals. The main one is ritual confession (Pali: *uposatha;* Sanskrit: *poshadha*), which takes place twice a month, at the new moon and the full moon. During the ceremony monks, and nuns recite the list of disciplinary rules and confess their faults in general terms. The aim of the ceremony is the ritual affirmation of purity and the cohesion of the order.

Young monks celebrating a Buddhist festival. Chiang Mai, Thailand. Before being ordained the candidate spends several years as a novice. Ordination usually occurs when the postulant is 13, but very young children are often entrusted to monasteries where they receive their education. Buddhist monasteries have long been educational as well as religious institutions.

Buddhism the triumph of secular aspirations. Conversely, it is possible to view it as return to the value that early Buddhism placed on the individual. As the Sangha developed this was sacrificed for the cohesion of the group and collective values. At the same time one should avoid overemphasizing the differences between the monastic community and the laity. If, on the whole, the laity were preoccupied with accumulating merit through good works and the monks were more concerned with their salvation, that was not always the case. Improving one's karma was one of the objectives of monastic practice as well. Moreover, in certain cases, ordination was perceived as the path to a comfortable sheltered existence. On the other hand some laics like Vimalakirti directed their full efforts towards liberation.

Certainly, in a number of schools ordination remained the sine qua non of

becoming an arhat, or Buddhist saint. But other schools recognized that this was possible for lay people as well. The possibility of transferring merit obtained by ritual or meditative practice detracted from the privileged position monks held in early Buddhism, in which each person was considered exclusively responsible for his own karma. To the extent that karma was considered the result of purely individual efforts, only those who had the leisure and the will to devote themselves to intense practice — that is monks and ascetics — could progress

The Body of the Buddha.
With its 32 primary marks, the body of the Buddha is a semiotic object, a sort of mandala that embodies Buddhist doctrine. This is particularly evident in the traditional representations of the soles of the Buddha's feet, which are marked with signs derived primarily from Hinduism. Although the body of the Buddha has been hidden or destroyed in nirvana, the traces of his footsteps can still be seen today. Tradition locates his footprints in many places, not only in India where he lived, but in China, Korea, and Japan.

toward liberation. Once merit was seen as being transferable from one individual (or group) to another, all became possible, and the distinctions between lay practitioners and the monastics blurred. Certain important laymen, in particular the kings from the time of the Buddha, became models for Buddhism. In renouncing the world, Shakyamuni had in fact preserved — or perhaps realized — the attributes of a universal monarch (*cakravartin*, literally "the king who turns the wheel"), as witnessed by the royal symbolism that permeated the celebrations of his final entrance into nirvana.

Novices at the Drepung Monastery, Tibet. The novice monk spends a number of years of apprenticeship studying Buddhist ritual and doctrine before receiving complete ordination (usually at age 18). At his ordination, he agrees to respect the 250 rules that constitute the disciplinary code of Buddhism. The five principal rules, observed by the laity as well, require Buddhists to refrain from killing, theft, illicit sexual acts, lying, and using intoxicants. If he wishes the monk may renounce his vows and return to a life in the world.

Schisms and Schools

The initial development of Indian Buddhism in the centuries following the disappearance of the Buddha were manifested in the proliferation of schools. The word "school" is a translation of the Sanskrit term *nikaya* (group). Diverging interpretations in matters of doctrine or discipline led to the founding of new schools. To avoid the pejorative appellation of the "Lesser Vehicle" (Hinayana), a term no doubt invented by adherents of the "Great Vehicle" (Mahayana), modern historians often call early Buddhism the Buddhism of the *nikaya*. But it seems ill advised to reduce this form of Buddhism

Ordination rites.
The ordination ceremonies for monks came to be modeled after the ritual of royal consecration. The unction with which the new sovereign is sprinkled comes from the four oceans, symbolizing his universal mastery. In contrast to the Western imagery of the two swords, temporal and spiritual, Buddhist ideology tends to harmonize the two aspects of Dharma, represented by the Buddha and the *cakravartin*, the clergy and the royal circle. This idea reached its pinnacle in medieval Japan.

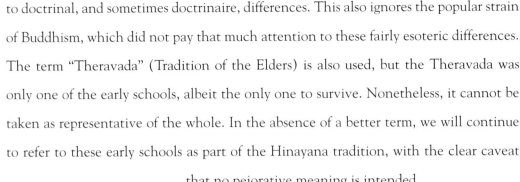

to doctrinal, and sometimes doctrinaire, differences. This also ignores the popular strain of Buddhism, which did not pay that much attention to these fairly esoteric differences. The term "Theravada" (Tradition of the Elders) is also used, but the Theravada was only one of the early schools, albeit the only one to survive. Nonetheless, it cannot be taken as representative of the whole. In the absence of a better term, we will continue to refer to these early schools as part of the Hinayana tradition, with the clear caveat that no pejorative meaning is intended.

Among the factors that contributed to the diversity of Indian Buddhism in the centuries following the death of the Buddha were the sedentary nature of monastic life and the great distances between Buddhist centers. As monasteries grew richer, monks were able to lead a more comfortable existence. This sometimes produced conflicts between the ascetics, who practiced in the solitude of the forest, and the monks of villages and towns who dedicated themselves to teaching or, in the great monasteries, to study.

Differences in doctrine, ritual, and discipline were sanctioned in the course of several councils. It was in the Third Council that the great schism occurred between the "Elder" (Pali: *thera*; Sanskrit: *Sthavira*), who insisted

Buddha in meditation. Taxila, Pakistan. One of the earliest forms of Buddhist art flourished in the Gandhara region. This style of art had many early Western admirers who saw in it the influence of classical Greek art. This led them to look upon the Buddha as an oriental Apollo.

Monasteries and the "paradox of holiness." One encounters the same paradox with the development of monastic orders in Europe during the Middle Ages. The more austere a monk was, the more he attracted donations, which jeopardized his austerity. Buddhist monks, who were not permitted to use these donations for their own profit, began to invest them or lend them out, becoming proto-capitalists.

Councils. It remains doubtful whether the first two councils — Rajagriha and Vaishali — ever took place. The existence of the Third Council is supported by historical evidence. It was held during the reign of Ashoka in the town of Pataliputa in North India.

on a literal interpretation of the Buddha's teaching, and the school called the "Great Assembly," *Mahasamghika*, a group that formed the majority at the council and sought to interpret the teachings according to the spirit rather than the letter. At the heart of this group was a movement that would crystallize into the Great Vehicle. The reason for the schism is somewhat surprising. It concerned a disagreement over the "five theses" of the monk Mahadeva on the nature of arhats, or Buddhist saints. He maintained that arhats could be subject to nocturnal emissions. This thesis could be seen as questioning the superhuman nature of the arhats or as a plea for the recognition of their humanity. Whatever the case, the controversy turned out to be just the opening shot of an attack on the practitioners of traditional Buddhism, who were accused of all manner of crimes, starting with incest. At the same time one should remember that Mahayana itself was a kind of heresy of Mahadeva: a paradoxical situation. The conservative faction, named Hinayana by its adversaries, also began to diversify. But even if there were schools within schools, the Chinese pilgrim Yijing, who visited India in the seventh century wrote: "Those who venerate Bodhisattvas and read the Mahayana sutras are called Mahayanists, the others call themselves Hinayanists." Monks of both orders lived together in the same

Wat Chai, Wattanaram, Ayutthaya, Thailand.

At bottom: *The Buddha's entry into final nirvana (parinirvana). Polonnaruwa, Sri Lanka. At the end of a life spent preaching his doctrine, the Buddha breathed his last in the town of Kushinagara in North India. The representation of this final episode of the Buddha's life became one of the principal images of Buddhist art.*

Schools.
Many schools existed at the time of the Third Council (tradition suggest eighteen but this number is probably symbolic). Today, only the teachings of the Theravada school exist and fragments of the doctrinal literature and the disciplinary code (Vinaya) of the Sarvastivadin and Dharmaguptaka schools have survived. The doctrines of the rest of the schools are now unknown. The importance of this proliferation of schools should not be overestimated, however. Doctrinal divisions, which are of interest to researchers, often mask the real evolution of Buddhism at the popular level.

monasteries. Moreover, most Indian Mahayanists followed Hinayana discipline (as was the case in China, Korea, and to a lesser extent Japan).

The Schools of Mahayana or the Great Vehicle

According to Vasumitra, author of a fourth century treatise on the origins of different Buddhist schools, all of them agreed in principle on the fundamental doctrine of the Four Noble Truths. Their controversies on the reality of time, the existence of phenomena, or the otherworldly nature of the buddhas, might appear somewhat byzantine to us. The analytic tendency reached its full fruition in the *Abhidharma-kosa,* a scholastic summa on the ninety-nine types of dharmas. With the Mahayana's emergence at the beginning of the common era, things took another turn. The question of the origin of Mahayana continues to vex scholars. Some attribute it to a reaction by the lay population against the elitism of the monks and their opulent way of life. Others emphasize the emergence of new forms of religiosity such as the cult of stupas and relics, or that of the scriptures, or more generally increased devotion to the figure of the Buddha. In fact, Mahayana seems to be a monastic phenomenon, militant in nature, even in some cases

Buddha seated on a lotus flower. Lahore Museum, Pakistan. The lotus, whose eight petals symbolize the directions, is a symbol of the cosmos.

Mahayana and violence.
It is no coincidence that the two Buddhist rebellions in China (sixth and seventh centuries) were instigated in the name of Mahayana, even if they were the actions of heterodox sects. In modern times, Mahayana Buddhism has taken militant forms, especially in Japan.

military, if one is to believe the *Parinirvana-sutra*: "If a lay person observes the five precepts but does not protect the monks by force of arms, he does not deserve the name of Mahayanist."

Despite all the polemics, Mahayana completed rather than nullified Hinayana teaching. As Etienne Lamotte has pointed out, it spread through insinuation, not revolution. One could speak of the secularization of the Buddhist clergy, but the opposition between the laity and the clergy was never as pronounced as in the West, and the influence of monasticism remained strong. If Mahayanist reform produced a certain laxity, it developed the ascetic tendencies of Buddhism at the same time and insisted on the virtues of wisdom, compassion, and skillful means.

Mahayana does radicalize certain ideas present in early Buddhism. Thus, the idea of the absence of self, which Hinayana applies only to the individual personality, is extended in the Mahayana to all phenomena. In its teachings on salvation, enlightenment assumes the central place held by nirvana in Hinayana. Concerning the figure of the Buddha one passes from a relative historicism to a radical docetism. The Buddha becomes entirely metaphysical, multiple Buddhas are postulated, and Shakyamuni's human appearance is regarded as no more than a pious lie to guide beings gradually to the truth. On a practical level, emphasis is placed on devotion to several buddhas (Amitabha, Akshobhya, Bhaishajyaguru, Vairocana) and bodhisattvas (Avalokiteshvara, Manjushri, Samantabhadra), as well as on penitence and the transfer of accumulated merit.

Head of the Buddha. Gandharan style, Victoria and Albert Museum, London. Before it was depicted in art, the Buddha's appearance was described in Buddhist texts that recount his 32 primary marks and 80 secondary marks. Among the primary marks are a cranial protuberance (ushnisha), elongated earlobes, eyebrows that meet between his eyes, and a tongue large enough to cover his face.

Mahayana.
One feature of Mahayana Buddhism is the "paradox of the bodhisattva." Bodhisattvas devote themselves to the salvation of all beings but at the same time recognize that all phenomena by their very nature are empty, lacking a fixed permanent reality. The paradox applies equally to the Bodhisattva's devotees, who display their faith in and gratitude toward a savior who teaches them that he is no more real than they.

The goddess Prajnaparamita, personification of the Perfection of Wisdom. Nalanda, India. In tantric Buddhism, the mystical union between the practitioner and the Perfection of Wisdom is represented symbolically as sexual union with the deity. She is known as Mother of all the Buddhas.

Mahayana thought began to mature with the tradition of the Perfection of Wisdom (*prajnaparamita*), which is explained and elaborated on in the sutras of the same name. The first of these texts appeared at the beginning of the common era. Their lengths varied from one extreme (recension in 100,000 verses) to another (recension called the *Heart of Perfect Wisdom*, about one page long). This literature is deliberately paradoxical, in that it drains all the teachings of earlier Buddhist schools of their content by maintaining the emptiness (*shunyata*) of all phenomena. The Middle Way as it is applied in the Perfection of Wisdom tradition is not simply a happy medium between asceticism and self-indulgence. It becomes a profoundly philosophical concept, the abandonment of all notions of being and nonbeing. Mahayana's resolutely anti-dualistic position goes so far as to reject the opposition between the extremes and the Middle Way itself.

The principal theses of the Perfection of Wisdom tradition were soon developed by the two most important schools of Mahayana Buddhism: Madhyamika — founded by Nagarjuna toward the beginning of the second century C.E. — and Yogacara (or Vijnanavada) — systematized by two brothers, Asanga (ca. 310–390) and Vasubhandu (ca. 320–400).

Nagarjuna was the theoretical genius behind the Perfection of Wisdom teaching. His logic of reductio ad absurdum, expressed in his *Fundamental Verses on the Middle Way (Mulamadhyamaka-karikah)*, ends with the classic definition of emptiness: "That which we call emptiness is conditioned origination. It is a conventional designation. It is equally the Middle Way." Emptiness, then, is simply the principle of relativity. One

Conventional and ultimate reality.
According to conventional truth, the Buddha attained enlightenment and entered into nirvana, leaving behind his teaching for future generations. This summarizes the essential of exoteric Buddhism, in which believers set out to practice the Buddha's teachings on the law of karma. According to the ultimate truth, the world is the body of the cosmic buddha Vairocana, and Shakyamuni only one manifestation among others of this primordial buddha. Every gesture, every sound, every sound is the gesture, sound, and thought of Vairocana, with whom the aspirant tries to identify. This is the essence of the teachings of esoteric Buddhism.

cannot concretize this theory more than that because the negation of all philosophical positions turns into a kind of nihilism. To go further, this negativity applies only to conventional reality: it does not imply the negation of an ultimate reality, beyond language. Nagarjuna, moreover, affirms the necessity of conventional reality as the means to access the ultimate reality. According to him reality is dialectical. Because things are intrinsically empty, they are interdependent.

Nagarjuna's best-known formulation consists of four propositions according to which one cannot affirm about any reality: (1) that it exists; (2) that it does not exist; (3) that it both exists and does not exist; or (4) that it neither exists nor does not exist. To the extent that one applies this formulation to nirvana as well as *samsara*, it is difficult to avoid the conclusion, which no doubt smacked of heresy to conservative Buddhists: "There exists not the slightest distinction between nirvana and *samsara*." These were presented in a veritable encyclopedia attributed to Nagarjuna and entitled the Upadesha, a commentary on the *Prajnaparamita-sutra* consisting of 25,000 articles. It was translated into Chinese in 416 by Kumarajiva.

About two centuries after Nagarjuna, Asanga

The entry of Buddha into final nirvana. Japanese scroll. Museum of Far Eastern Art, Cologne, Germany.

Tathagatagarbha.
The ideas formulated by Asanga and Vasubhandu provoked the elaboration of other theories, which, if they did not lead to the founding of schools, nonetheless exercised considerable influence on the development of Mahayana Buddhism. The most important of their ideas was the concept of *tathagatagarbha* — "womb" or "embryo" (the term *garbha* has two senses) of the *tathagata* (a synonym for the Buddha, meaning "Thus gone"). This may be held to indicate the awakening power within each of us, the Buddha nature in every sentient being. This notion has played a guiding role in Tibetan Buddhism as well as in the Chan/Zen school.

The bodhisattva Samantabhadra in sexual union with his shakti (consort). Tibetan silk painting, Maraini collection, Florence. This union symbolizes the complementarity of the principles of compassion (karuna) and wisdom (prajna).

and Vasubhandu proposed a new way of looking at the question of emptiness. They and their followers of the Vijnanavada school put forth the concept of Mind Only, that is that the external world is a product of mind. They distinguished eight types of awareness. The first six are associated with the five senses and thought. The seventh, *manas*, is the individualized consciousness. The eighth is "deep awareness" *(alaya-vijnana)*, a sort of collective unconscious containing the seeds of all past actions, which will come to full bloom in the future.

Vajrayana or Tantrism

In the fifth century a new ritual and doctrinal movement appears. Perceived by some as the ultimate development of Mahayana Buddhism, by others as a third "turning of the Wheel of Dharma," or as an entirely new vehicle, it was called Vajrayana, a term that translates as the "Way of the Thunderbolt" or the "Way of the Diamond". This movement was based upon a type of text called "tantra". On a philosophical level, Vajrayana inherited the ideas of Mahayana and pushed them to their ultimate conclusion. The oneness of nirvana and *samsara*, in particular, formed the basis of tantric doctrine and practice. This oneness was unequivocally observed. According to

Tantra.
Tantric teachings were a reform movement that originally affected Hinduism as well as Buddhism. Somewhat later on tantra also became known as Mantrayana, or "vehicle of mantras" (ritual incantations).

Sexual symbolism.
The non-dualistic philosophy of Mahayana is concretely translated as a union of opposites, often sexual in nature. This may pertain to the union of deities or of the adept and his partner. This union is also represented by symbols such as the sun and the moon, by the colors red and white, and phonetically by the combination of consonants and vowels that form mantras and invocations *(dharani)*.

this approach, all physical, verbal, or mental actions become the acts of the primordial Buddha. This identification of the human body with the Buddha opened the door to all kinds of transgressions. Thus, certain tantric adepts came to look upon illicit behavior — sex, intoxication, theft, even murder — as means or expressions of liberation.

Tantra makes great use of symbols of all sorts: vocalizations (mantras, *dharana*), gestures (mudras), and imagery (mandalas). Its reliance on ritual is the element that most clearly distinguishes it from early forms of Buddhism. Another important facet of tantra is its emphasis on the transmutation of negative energies, symbolized by sometimes terrifying deities that the practitioner visualizes during meditation. Unlike other Buddhists, followers of the Vajrayana school are not content simply to invoke deities to venerate at a distance; they seek to ritually identify themselves with the deity.

Magical powers are considered important in tantra. Although these play a role in most forms of traditional Buddhism, only tantra looks upon them as unqualifiedly positive.

Despite its radical nature, tantric Buddhism was quickly institutionalized, becoming one monastic discipline among others that could be studied in Buddhist universities such as Nalanda.

Hevajra, tantric deity. Tibetan tangka, 18th century, detail from a wall painting. Sagya, Tibet.

At bottom, pages 30 and 31: Wrathful deities. Details from wall paintings. Sagya, Tibet.

The Sahajiya saints. In reaction to tantric practice's becoming routine, the Sahajiya saints affirmed the value of transgression. Their iconoclastic and eccentric behavior, which they sometimes carried to the point of madness, was made much of in Buddhist chronicles. But these exceptional individuals remained just that, exceptions that proved the general rules of the Buddhist codes of discipline and right action.

Tibetan lamas. Nepal. The term "lama" is a translation of the Sanskrit "guru" (literally, "weighty"), designating a person of spiritual substance. In tantric practice, the guru is considered to be a Fourth Jewel in addition to the Buddha, the Dharma, and the Sangha. The aspirant can reach the truth through devotion to the guru.

On the doctrinal level the traditional division of Buddhism into three separate waves — Hinayana, Mahayana and Vajrayana — has the disadvantage of forcing one to overlook the broad and enduring similarities among them. It also can lead to value judgments based upon arguments from hindsight or teleology. Following the model most widespread, today Hinayana is an ethical (almost Kantian) system that affirms the autonomy of the individual and rejects all forms of ritualism.

Compared to this original, pure form of Buddhism, Mahayana and to an even greater extent Vajrayana are pietist deviations, consumed with ritual and often morally lax. A second model, characteristic of Sino-Japanese studies, looks at the ethical system propounded by Hinayana and finds it rather sterile and self-congratulatory. By contrast, Mahayana, especially the Pure Land school, is more authentic and democratic. A

variant of this reasoning is used to explain the evolution of Buddhism in Japan — the more or less Hinayana schools of the Nara period developed into the tantrism of the Heian period, to culminate in the new popular Buddhism of the Kamakura period. A third model is used by those who consider Vajrayana to be the summit of Buddhist thought. They chart a process that begins with the individual austerities of the Hinayana school, develops into the emphasis on compassion in Mahayana, which promises salvation in some distant future, to the

The great stupa of Swayambhunath. Kathmandu, Nepal. The open eyes painted on all four sides signify the vigilant presence of the Buddha.

superior Vajrayana path to liberation , by which one can become a buddha "even in this body" (that is, in one's present lifetime). None of these evolutionary models suffice to retrace the complex history of Buddhism. It remains pluralistic, defying any linear simplification.

The reasons for the decline of Buddhism in India are many. Socioeconomic factors made Buddhism vulnerable, dependent on political support. In addition, a divide grew up between the monks and the laity, because of the high-handedness of the great monasteries, which had become major financial entities. Buddhism also had to face a revival of Hinduism (notably, cults devoted to Vishnu and Shiva). The final blow came with the Muslim invasions (first from Arabia and then from Turkey). The destruction of the university at Nalanda, a major cultural and religious center, brought down the curtain on Buddhism in India.

Divinity with peacock, tantric figure. Painted scroll, first half of 12th century, Tokyo. The peacock is a symbol of protection.

The Wheel of Time. One of the last-ditch efforts of Buddhism to respond to the challenge thrown down by the Muslim invasion of East Asia was the production of a text entitled *The Wheel of Time* (*Kalacakra-tantra*), It called for a kind of holy war against the Muslim interlopers under the leadership of Kalkin Cakrin, a Buddhist version of Kalki, the tenth, apocalyptic incarnation of Vishnu. But in the realm of holy wars, Buddhists (and Indians in general) were not really at their best. In addition, as if frightened by its own audacity, the text in question ends by interpreting the idea of holy war as a metaphor for the battle of wisdom against ignorance. The tradition of the *Kalacakra-tantra* has nonetheless survived to the present day.

Expansion into Asia

The expansion of Buddhism in Asia within India's cultural sphere took place in three major phases: the introduction of Buddhism into Sri Lanka (and no doubt Southeast Asia as well) under the reign of Ashoka; the Theravadan reforms of the eleventh and twelfth centuries; and the Anglo-French colonial occupations of the seventeenth and eighteenth centuries.

If Mahayana and Vajrayana had for a long time been the main forms of the religion in the many lands of Southeast Asia, as evidenced by the grandeur of monuments such as Pagan in Burma, Angkor in Cambodia, and Borobudur in Indonesia, from the tenth century onward the Theravadan tradition became dominant. Theravada, or the Way of the Ancients, represents the conservative tendency in Buddhism. Its traditions, transmitted orally for many generations, came to be centered around the Mahavihara ("Great Monastery") in the capital of Sri Lanka between the third and fifth centuries of our era. From there it expanded into Burma around 1,000 C.E. and through the rest of Indochina in the centuries that followed.

The Spread of Theravada

According to tradition, it was during the reign of Ashoka (third century B.C.E.) that Buddhism first reached Sri Lanka. King Devanampiya-tissa (r. 250–210 B.C.E.) is said to have been converted by Ashoka's own son, from whom he received relics of the Buddha.

Early expansion. Buddhism expanded early on along with the spread of Indian culture into Burma, Thailand, and Laos. In these places, kings had Sanskrit names. The cult of the "divine king" (*devaraja*), for example, was introduced into Angkor in the ninth century. This holy city was the home to such composite gods as Lokeshvara (a cross between the bodhisattva Avalokiteshvara and the Hindu god Shiva).

In Indonesia, the cosmic stupa of Borobudur represented at once Mount Sumeru at the center of the universe, the body of the cosmic Buddha, and royal power. But the rapid rise of tantric Hinduism and then the country's conversion to Islam in the 15th century brought an end to this brilliant culture.

Opposite page: *Angkor. Cambodia provides the best example of the integration of Buddhism with the cult of the state. The temples of Angkor, concealed for centuries by the jungle, were both sacred mountains and royal tombs. The majestic faces that adorn the four sides of their towers depict the traits of the king and syncretic god Lokeshvara.*

Below: *Ruwanweli Stupa, Sri Lanka.*

Bas-relief, Angkor. Probably a local deity that has been assimilated into the Buddhist pantheon.

These he placed inside the great temple of Mahavihara that he had just built in his capital, Anuradhapura. For a long time, Theravada coexisted with Mahayana, which was centered in the Abhayagiri monastery. Gradually, a secular rivalry grew up between the two monasteries. In the eighth century, the Vajrayana tradition made its way onto the island as well and soon became quite popular. Finally, following a period of internal reformation, the Theravada school won over the others. Soon it had taken root in most of the kingdoms of Southeast Asia.

During the period of rivalry between the various monasteries on the island, the Theravadan Buddhists set down their scriptures in writing, composing what is now known as the Pali canon. During the fifth and sixth centuries, several great teachers and scholars appeared, among whom was Buddhagosa, author of a veritable *Summa Theologica* of Buddhism, entitled "The Path of Purification" (*Visuddhi-magga*), which would define orthodox Theravadan Buddhism for centuries to come.

With the arrival of the Thais in the Indochinese peninsula in the fourteenth century, Theravadan Buddhism began to diversify. One consistent trait was the importance of monasticism. Ordination was a rite that all young people had to go through. Paradoxically, this "departure from the family" served to preserve the institution of the family. Monasteries became pedagogic centers, where adolescents acquired the discipline that they would need as adults. Buddhism became the official religion of Thailand, the doctrine that guided (or was supposed to guide) the moral conduct of the nation. The king and the Sangha maintained close relations, and monks were often embroiled in politics: some of them were even kingmakers. At the same time,

Buddhism in Vietnam. Vietnam received the teachings of Theravada Buddhism at the beginning of the common era. It was not until some centuries later that it received from China several forms of Mahayana, including the Chan (Vietnamese: Thien) and Pure Land schools. The role that Buddhist monks played in protesting the Vietnam war by their suicides is well known.

the king played an important role in the evolution of the monastic community.

Theravada thus provided a common culture and religion for the kingdoms of Asia that were once under Indian influence. The spread of Pali as a lingua franca simply increased its importance. Throughout, the historical Buddha was the principal object of veneration, but his worship was often interwoven with preexisting local cults. Theravada was not always as free from mystical and esoteric elements as is generally supposed. There existed in addition a tantric form of Theravada, which was deeply imbued with mystical speculations.

Tibetan Buddhism

In spite of its critique of traditional Buddhism, Vajrayana remained fairly conservative. With a few important exceptions, it was quickly assimilated and became an integral part of Buddhism in India. Have reached its high-water mark in the seventh century, it spread into Tibet, China, and Japan. In Tibet, it was imposed as the state religion. In the countries of the Far East, it was transmitted in a purified form (that is, purged of its most flagrantly sexual elements). Under the name *mikkyo*

The bodhisattva Avalokiteshvara, surrounded by lamas and divinities. Tibetan tangka, 19th century, Maraini collection, Florence. Bodhisattva are enlightened beings who guide others to nirvana before entering into it themselves.

Tibetan Buddhism in the West.
Because of political circumstances that forced substantial numbers of the Tibetan people into exile in 1959, Tibetan Buddhism has become one of the most understood (and misunderstood) Buddhist traditions in the West. Its attraction lies in certain tantric characteristics, particularly its symbolic richness and its aesthetic character. Tibet has always occupied an important place in the European imagination, as witnessed by the myth of Shangri-la. The mystique of the Dalai Lama has also contributed to this state of affairs.

The Wheel of Dharma. Jokhang Temple, Lhasa, Tibet. The Buddha was often represented in symbolic form: as a stupa, the Wheel of Dharma, an empty seat, or by a set of footprints.

Below: *Tenzin Gyatso, the 14th Dalai Lama. Tibetan Buddhists regard the Dalai Lama as the incarnation of the bodhisattva Avalokiteshvara.*

("secret doctrine"), it became the dominant form of Japanese Buddhism.

Despite its proximity to India Tibet remained unaffected by either Buddhism or Hinduism for many centuries. Although Buddhist doctrine had spread as far as Central Asia and China at the beginning of the common era, it did not officially arrive in Tibet until the seventh century under the reign of King Songtsen Gampo (r. 620–649). Three major phases of Buddhism's expansion into Tibet can be delineated, corresponding to its establishment in the seventh century, its reformation starting in the ninth century, and the installation of the line the Dalai Lamas in the seventeenth century. These phases are marked by the rapid development of the main Tibetan schools of Buddhism: the Nyingmapa (or "Ancients"), the Sakyapa (named after Sakya, their principal monastery), the Kagyupa (adepts of the oral tradition), and the Gelukpa (the "Virtuous"). Until the Chinese takeover in 1950 the Dalai Lamas reigned in spiritual and temporal matters throughout Tibet, and the Gelukpa order was dominant.

A few words ought to be said about *Bön* (or *Bönpo*). Originally, the term was applied to local cults that practiced animal sacrifice. The religion that sprang up in the eleventh century under this name significantly differed from these earlier cults. It was strongly influenced by the new Buddhist schools, and particularly the older Nyingmapa school. Nonetheless, it rejected the authority of the historical Buddha, Shakyamuni, replacing

Theocracy.
From the 17th century until modern times, Tibet was cloistered in a kind of medieval theocracy. But the forces of history, which seemed to have stopped in Lhasa, made themselves felt once again with the British invasion of Tibet in 1904

during the reign of the 13th Dalai Lama. In 1909, the Manchus launched an attack, and the Dalai Lama had to flee to India. He returned to Tibet in 1911 and tried to undertake reforms but did not succeed. A year after his death in 1934, a new Dalai Lama,

Tenzin Gyatso, was found. He was only 14 years old when the Chinese invaded Tibet in 1950. After unsuccessful efforts at comprimise, he fled Tibet for India in 1959.

him with an earlier Buddha whose doctrine they claimed was repressed by Buddhism. For the practitioners of Bön, Buddhism was a detestable heresy, though this did not prevent them from developing institutions whose similarities to those of Buddhism recall the relations between Buddhism and Taoism in China and Shintoism in Japan.

Chinese and Japanese Buddhism

The expansion of Buddhism into the Far East resulted in profound changes from its original Indian model. Central Asia played an important part in this transformation through the transmission of religions from the Middle East: Zoroastrianism, Manichaeism, and Christianity. The oases on the Silk Route became flourishing cultural centers. When Buddhism was first introduced into China at the beginning of our ear, it was taken for a form of Taoism, the established religion whose legendary founder was Laozi.

From the fourth century on, the differences between the two became increasingly evident and their rivalry more acute. The controversy culminated with the Taoist doctrine of "the conversion of the barbarians by Laozi." Though in appearance rather trivial, a battle was being played for high stakes and continued for hundreds of

Wall painting, Mogao Cave, Dunhuang, China. The oasis of Dunhuang was the last stage on the Silk Route before reaching China. Somewhere around the 11th century thousands of manuscripts in Tibetan, Chinese, and other Asian languages were deposited there. It was not until this century that they were recovered.

The Legend of Laozi. At the end of his life Laozi, in the guise of the Buddha, was said to have departed to the west to convert the barbarians. To punish them for their initial lack of faith, he condemned them to celibacy. Thus the legend proposes that Buddhism is no more than an adulterated version of Taoism, one suited to the barbarians, and that the Chinese were the actual originators of the religion. The Buddhists countered by maintaining that Laozi and Confucius (the other great Chinese sage) were actually disciples of the Buddha, sent by him to convert the Chinese and prepare the way for the arrival of Buddhist doctrine. The controversy lasted for centuries but was finally resolved with the defeat of Taoism.

Buddhist temple in Hwaomsa, Cholla Pukdo Province, South Korea. This complex of wooden buildings was constructed during the Yi dynasty, which lasted from 1392 until the Japanese occupation of Korea in 1910. Wooden pavilions stand on stone platforms.

years. It was not until the end of the twelfth century that the dispute ended with the unequivocal victory of Buddhism.

In the course of its transplantation into Chinese soil, Buddhism had to face many other challenges, notably the question of monastic autonomy. In contrast to India where the clergy (whether Hindu or Buddhist) held undisputed sway over all spiritual matters, in China the emperor, who was called the Son of Heaven, enjoyed a celestial mandate.

He was at the pinnacle of both the temporal and spiritual hierarchies, and monks had to submit to his decrees. Their allegiance was not, however, easily given or retained. Numerous monastic pamphlets declared that monks should not be required to prostrate to the emperor. But the battle was lost before it ever really began: from the fifth century onward, Buddhism was tamed and integrated into the imperial apparatus. The emperors were not looking for this foreign religion to deliver them from this world. They wanted it to increase their power in it. Of the diverse schools that sprang up during the Tang dynasty (7th to 10th centuries), the tantric school of Zhen'yan (literally "true words," or mantras) best served these imperial ambitions.

Despite its great success in China, Buddhism has always borne the stigma of a foreign religion and has

Buddhism in Korea. Although strongly influenced by China, Buddhism in Korea nonetheless developed its own character quite early on. After flourishing under Silla and Koguryo, Buddhism was eclipsed by Confucianism during the Yi dynasty. After the Japanese occupation in 1910, Japanese forms of Buddhism made themselves felt, but with the end of World War II, homegrown practices and beliefs reasserted themselves despite the growing popularity of Christianity. At present, the various Korean sects have united under the aegis of the Chogye school, a Korean form of Chan.

periodically been the object of state-sponsored persecutions. In 845, during the reign of the emperor Wuzong, more than two thousand monks and nuns were defrocked, and many temples and religious monuments were destroyed. In our own time, the Cultural Revolution left deep scars. But Buddhism has become too embedded in the Chinese psyche to be dislodged.

The evolution of Buddhism in Japan has been altogether different. Soon after its introduction in Japan in the sixth century, it became the official religion under the enlightened rule of Emperor Shotoku (574–622). During the Nara period, the capital could boast of magnificent temples such as Todaiji, where a colossal statue of Vairocana, the celestial Buddha, was consecrated in 753. In fact, it was to escape from the increasingly powerful hold monks exercised, expressed in an attempted usurpation of the throne by Dokyo, that the emperor decided to move to a new capital, Heiankyo. But since the new capital could not be founded without Buddhism's protection and sanction, the emperor called upon two monks recently returned from China, Saicho and Kukai. With imperial support, these two masters founded the two sects that would come to dominate the Heian period, Tendai and Shingon.

In the Kamakura period, new reform movements such as Zen, Pure Land, and Nichiren appeared. Their doctrinal radicalism notwithstanding, these schools fit into the ideological frame constructed by the traditional schools of the preceding period. They too were based on tantric doctrine. It was not until the end of the medieval period in the sixteenth century that that system fell apart, permitting new, more radical religious tendencies to emerge and express themselves in popular uprisings. After the

Pagoda of the Songyue Monastery (founded in 523 C.E. under the Northern Wei dynasty). This five-story structure is made of bricks and is the oldest surviving pagoda in China. Situated on Mount Song, the "Central Mountain," one of the five sacred mountains in China, the Songyue Monastery along with the neighboring monastery of Shaolin, was one of the earliest centers of the Chan sect. According to tradition, Bodhidharma, the first patriarch of Chan, settled on here at the beginning of the sixth century.

The evolution of the stupa in China.
Originally stupas were hemispheric, in the shape of an overturned bowl. They were essentially mausoleums containing the relics of the Buddha (Sanskrit: *sharira* or *dhatu*). The term *dagoba* (probably an abbreviation of *dhatugarbha*, reliquary) used in Sri Lanka evolved into the word "pagoda". Superficially, the pagoda seems far from the stupa, but there is no doubt that the former derives from the latter. This transformation occurred in China and Japan, with the addition of different levels with curved roofs, following Chinese geomantic beliefs.

Rock sculptures of Yungang, China. In the sixth century, enthusiasm for Buddhism culminated in an outpouring of monumental sculpture carved in rock at sites such as Yungang and Longmen. The themes represented attest to the importance of Maitreya, the buddha of the future.

repression of these revolts and the reunification of Japan under the Tokugawa shoguns, Buddhism was enshrined as the official ideology, and popular religious sentiments, impregnated with millennial ideas, were pushed to the margins, where they developed as the "new religions" of the end of the Edo period (1603–1867). The Meiji restoration in 1868, marked the end of an epoch for Buddhism in Japan. It was abruptly relegated to the status of "foreign religion," and Shintoism, the new national religion, took its place.

Forced to return to greater doctrinal purity, to "separate the *kamis* from the Buddhas" (*kamis* were indigenous deities), the Buddhism of the Meiji period sought to recapture its great past by returning to the various doctrinal (and sectarian) positions that had characterized the Kamakura period. This clear perception of Buddhism as consisting of completely distinct sects belies the syncretism of popular Buddhism, but it is the version that prevailed.

Tantric Buddhism in China and Japan

As Michel Strickmann has pointed out: "Tantric rituals and institutions served as the primary vehicle for the transmission of Indian culture throughout Asia. This was especially the case in Japan." At the beginning of the

The marriage of Shintoism and Buddhism. Buddhism was very successful at assimilating local religions. This syncretism took its most systematic form in Japan. Numerous Shinto-Buddhist cults arose, many of which are still in existence despite the official separation of the two religions under the Meiji dynasty. Accordingly, the Japanese kamis — spirits representing the hidden forces of nature as well as the souls of the living and the dead — are considered to be traces, or local manifestations of Indian buddhas. The best-known example is that of the solar deity Amaterasu, the most important Japanese divinity. Her name means "the Illuminator of the Heavens." Buddhists quickly realized that they could profit by this

Tang dynasty, Chinese Buddhism already contained tantric elements, but it was not until the beginning of the eighth century that Vajrayana, as a school, was introduced in China under the name of Zhen'yan ("School of Mantras"). It was brought to China by the Indian tantric masters Shubhakarasimha (Chinese: Shanwuwei, 637–735 C.E.), Vajrabodhi (Chinese: Jingangzhi, 671–741 C.E.), and Amoghavajra (Chinese: Bukong, 705–774 C.E.). The last mentioned exercised a great influence on the emperor Xuanzong, and for a time Zhen'yan was accepted as the orthodox version of Chinese Buddhism, but it soon ran up against Confucian anticlericalism. Unlike the Chan and Pure Land, schools it never regained its former position after the anti-Buddhist persecutions of 845. But tantric Buddhism did not disappear as quickly or as completely from China as has often been supposed. It was reintroduced in its Tibetan form when the Mongols took power in the thirteenth century. It was this form that Marco Polo encountered. In addition, some tantric ideas were taken up by popular religions, notably Taoism. This should come as no surprise, since there are numerous points of convergence between tantric and Taoist sexual practices, particularly evident in their teachings on alchemy and the "art of preserving the vital essence." Both religions were the object of similar attacks by the

Painted scroll, 13th century, Ichijoji, Hyogo, Japan. The Indian monk Shubhakarasimha introduced tantric practice in China at the beginning of the eighth century. His disciple, the Chinese monk Yixing, was known for his scientific discoveries.

etymology by emphasizing that the name of the cosmic Buddha, Vairocana (Japanese: Dainichi) means "Great Sun." To conclude from this that Amaterasu was simply a local manifestation of Dainichi was only a brief step, and one that was quickly taken.

The same logic was soon extended to other *kamis*, all of whom became forms of various buddhas and bodhisattvas. The strict devotees of Shintoism reacted against this amalgam, and in 1868 Shintoism became the official religion of imperial

Japan. After the Japanese defeat in World War II, Shintoism lost its privileged position, but the separation between the two religions remains impressed in institutional structures.

Buddhist celestial hierarchies. Painted scroll, 19th century, Ichijoji, Hyogo, Japan.

At bottom: *Kobo Daishi (Kukai), founder of the Shingon sect. Sculpture in lacquered wood. Museé Guimet, Paris.*

Confucianists, who sought to eradicate magic and superstition. But the Confucianist ideologues underestimated the Chinese sovereigns' fascination with spiritual and magical powers.

The historians of Japanese Buddhism prefer the word "esotericism" (*mikkyo*) to distinguish their "pure" tantric practices (stripped of all sexual and magical elements) from the "impure" Indo-Tibetan form. But this distinction is more ideological than substantial and should not be allowed to mask the continuity between the two movements. Tantric Buddhism was introduced in Japan by Kukai. Legends quickly grew up around this personage, who is better known in popular religion by his posthumous title, Kobo Daishi. The esoteric doctrine of Shingon, transmitted and elaborated by Kukai, had a significant influence on the entire Heian period. It was based upon a collection of rites concerning the two great mandalas: the womb-pattern mandala (Sanskrit: Garbhadhatu; Japanese: Taizokai) and the diamond-pattern mandala (Sanskrit: Vajradhatu; Japanese: Kongokai), which represent the two complementary and non-dualistic aspects of reality, the two principles behind all manifestation. The universe, which is nothing other than the body of the cosmic Buddha, Vairocana, consists

Kukai.
Kukai is credited with founding a multitude of temples and monasteries in addition to those that he really did found: Kongobuji (on Mount Koya in 816) and Toji (in the capital in 823). Tradition also has it that he invented the *kana* system of Japanese writing, a syllabary based on a simplification of Chinese characters and their phonetic use according to a variant of Sanskrit. But the best-known part of his legend is his entry into *samadhi* .(in other words his death followed by mummification) in a cave on Mount Koya in 835. This ritual death, which was perceived as a sort of catalepsy was the result of a vow that Kukai took to imitate Mahakashyapa, the disciple of the Buddha who entered the state of *samadhi* to await the coming of

of five elements (earth, water, fire, air, and space), which are symbolized by the five levels, or wheels, of the stupas, or the five revolutions of the Sanskrit letter *siddham* ("a"), the source of all sounds and thus all things.

Another important aspect of Shingon doctrine is the idea that one can "become a Buddha even in this body" (*sokushin jobutsu*). This theory explains the mummification of Kukai, indisputable proof to his disciples that he had attained buddhahood. This apotheosis is possible because of the essential identity of the Buddha with all created beings. Tantric meditation consists in precisely this: ritually identifying oneself with the Buddha Vairocana. One must realize the "three mysteries," in other words, imitate the acts of Vairocana — acts of the body (particularly *mudras*, symbolic gestures), speech (through mantras or incantations), and thought (through contemplation of mandalas).

Soon, under the influence of Shingon, all the other schools of Japanese Buddhism, beginning with Tendai, became more esoteric. The importance of esoteric art and symbolism was particularly pronounced in medieval Japan. Another important doctrine was the theory called "real nature and its traces," (*honji suijaku*), which permitted indigenous deities (*kamis*, the spirits of

Mandala of the Shingon school. Ninth century, Gokukuji, Kyoto, Japan. This mandala, called the diamond-pattern mandala" represents along with the womb-pattern mandala the two complementary aspects of existence.

Maitreya, the buddha of the future. Faith in Kukai's supernatural powers quickly transformed the vicinity of his mausoleum into a vast cemetery. His followers would demand to have their ashes laid to rest there to ensure their rebirth in Maitreya's paradise.

Buddhist monk. Wood Sculpture, Museum of Oriental Art, Rome. Buddhist iconography is characterized by mudras, ritual gestures that express certain aspects of the Dharma and identify the aspirant with the Buddha. This Buddhist monk (or perhaps bodhisattva) is shown in the mudras of compassion and protection.

Japanese folk religion, were considered "traces") to be assimilated by or identified with the original (Indian) buddhas, who are their "real nature."

Chan/Zen and Pure Land Schools

Faithful to the idea that there are two truths (conventional and ultimate), tantric Buddhism emphasized the importance of magical powers as much as awakening. By contrast, Chan/Zen held unswervingly to the sole ultimate truth and in so doing eschewed all conventional aspects of religious practice (and all ritual and magical elements including images, prayers, and incantations). Buddhism of the Pure Land school, on the other hand, concentrated on the purely devotional aspects of the religion, affirming that a buddha who was indeed real (if also metaphysical) would save those who called upon him.

Zen/Chan and Pure Land Buddhism are often held to be representative of two opposing principles, that in Japanese are called *jiriki* (the idea that an individual's salvation depends on his own efforts) and *tariki* (the idea that salvation can be obtained only through the power of another, in the form of Amitabha/Amida). All the same, the two schools had much in common. They both attempted to reform Buddhism by simplifying it, and they emphasized practice over theory, even to the extent of advocating just one practice from the arsenal of spiritual techniques that had been developed over the course of Buddhist history. The explosive development of both schools at the beginning of the Tang dynasty can be explained by the religious context

Shugendo.
In the ninth century, a symbolic and ritual system called Shugendo arose in Japan. The followers of this cult looked upon mountains as the primary objects (and sites) of their practice. To them, the mountain was the definitive holy place, land of the dead and body of the gods. It was also seen as a three-dimensional mandala, or a Pure Land. Mountain climbing was seen as a return to the source or the womb, a kind of death and initiation and an ascension to paradise. In their ascetic practices in the mountains, the adepts of Shugendo sought to purify themselves and undergo rebirth. In the process they could acquire magical and psychic powers. They thereby established a reputation as doctors of the body and spirit, healers and exorcists,

of the time. Buddhism arrived in China in fragments, finally becoming the product of several syntheses, of which the most successful was that of Zhiyi (538–597), the founder of the Tiantai school (Japanese: Tendai). But the resulting synthesis of all the doctrines and practices of Indian Buddhism was exceedingly complex. If it satisfied the intellectual elites, its very perfection put off ordinary people. That is why certain contemporaries of Zhiyi sought to retain among the numerous meditation practices classified under the rubric of the "four *samadhi*" only those that seemed the simplest. From these four samadhis Chan espoused the first (sitting meditation), the Pure Land school, the second (based on the ambulatory recitation of the name of Buddha Amitabha). Thus, though the practices were different, the intent was the same: simplification leading to *samadhi* through a single practice.

Chan/Zen is said to owe its establishment to the legendary Bodhidharma, an Indian monk who arrived in China at the beginning of the sixth century. Retrospectively, he became known as the first "Chinese" patriarch of the new school. But it was not until the time of the fourth and fifth patriarchs, Daoxin and Hongren, that Chan imposed itself as orthodoxy. At the beginning of the eighth century, the school separated into two

who were both sought out and feared. This form of tantric practice, deeply imbued with the beliefs of local cults, is specific to Japanese Buddhism. After a long eclipse it is now the object of awakening interest.

Cave of Bodhidharma. Shaolin Monastery, China. In this cave, the Indian monk practiced meditation.

Below: *Kongo ban, 12th century, National Museum, Tokyo. Ritual object of Shingon Buddhism, it is the image of the* vajra, *(thunderbolt), emblem of this school.*

Portrait of the Chinese poet Li Bo by Liang Kai. Ink on paper, National Museum, Tokyo.

At bottom: Zen calligraphy. Ink on paper, Nojiri Michiko collection, Rome.

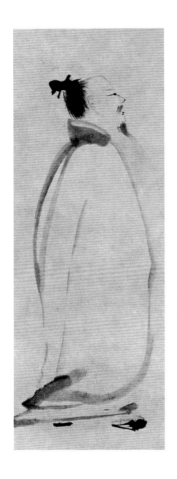

branches, northern and southern, over the controversy concerning "sudden enlightenment." In the following century, the southern branch further divided into five branches, although in contrast to the earlier controversy none of these sects was viewed as heterodox. Only two branches survived into the Song dynasty, the Linji and Caodong lines. These were brought into Japan during the Kamakura period under the Japanese names of Rinzai and Soto. Tradition credits the transmission to two Japanese monks, Eisai (1141–1215) and Dogen (1200–1253). In fact, Zen had already reached Japanese shores during the Heian period, arriving as an integral part of the Tendai school, before giving birth at the end of the twelfth century to the school of Bodhidharma (Darumashu). Unfortunately, this school was the subject of harsh critiques not only by Tendai monks but by Eisai and Dogen as well, and it was soon erased from the official version of Zen history.

Beginning in the fourteenth century, Zen began to occupy a central place in Japanese life, becoming the official ideology of the shoguns, the warrior elite who controlled Japan from their eastern capital, Kamakura. The great Zen monasteries, collectively referred to as the five mountains (*gozan*), played a key diplomatic role in relations with China, as well as a cultural role in spreading Chinese culture. Their success was noticed by the first Jesuit missionaries to Japan, who were astonished at the difference in the respect accorded the clergy in China and Japan.

Another characteristic of Zen, particularly in the Rinzai tradition, is its aesthetic tendency. The enthusiasm for Zen arts such as the tea ceremony, flower arrangement, rock gardens, calligraphy, and drawing is well known.

Zen.
In Japan one often hears expressions such as "Zen and poetry are one and the same" or "Zen and tea have the same taste." One could go on at length about the guiding role of Zen in Japanese art. This perspective owes a great deal to certain popular writers such as D. T. Suzuki, an adept of the Rinzai branch, who made it better known in the West but at the same time tended to reduce all of Japanese culture to Zen. In reality, Zen has always been part of the elite culture, while popular culture, which greatly influenced the development of Buddhism (including Zen), is passed over in silence. [transmission in Chan/zen]

Let us finish with a few words about the doctrine of Chan/Zen. The controversy over sudden enlightenment that divided Chan in the eighth century did not concern whether awakening came suddenly so much as whether it was the result of good works or contemplative techniques. Whereas the northern school underlined the utility of certain practices, the southern school rejected them entirely. The two positions are clearly illustrated in a story about a poetry contest in which the founders of the divergent branches, Shenxiu and Huineng, competed. Shenxiu offered: "The body is the tree of awakening/Mind is like a clear mirror/Apply yourself ceaselessly to polishing it/So that no dust can settle upon it." To which Huineng replied: "There is no tree of awakening/No mirror/In truth nothing exists/What can there be found for dust to settle upon?"

It is this poem that elevated Huineng to the position of sixth patriarch. Unfortunately, the two poems are apocryphal and the whole story is likely the creation of Huineng's disciples. This doctrine, according to which all practices are unnecessary, because everything is empty, leads to a logical impasse. If all beings are intrinsically awakened, then sitting meditation is as useless as good works, and Chan and all its patriarchs forfeit their entire reason for being. As the Chan master Linji Yixuan unequivocally remarks: "The important thing is not to be distracted: to eat and drink, piss and shit." In practice, however, this

The sixth patriarch cutting a bamboo stalk. Painting by Liang Kai, early 13th century, National Museum, Tokyo. Chan Buddhism, as it evolved in China in the sixth century, was characterized by a return to the concrete and the abandonment of contemplative quietism and the scholarly pursuits of traditional Buddhism. Chan monasteries emphasized daily work. In the words of one patriarch: "A day without work is like a day without food." This image expresses this new attitude.

radicalism was quickly moderated.

Classic Chan continued nonetheless to maintain itself through a unique tradition that could not be passed down in writing, since it was founded on the special unwritten transmission from one mind to another. Its practices penetrated directly into the mind and permitted the aspirant to see his own buddha-nature and become buddha. This explains the importance of the relationship between master and disciple and of the line of transmission. Ultimately, it is the legitimacy of the lineage that guarantees the authenticity of the practice and not the other way around (as is traditionally the case in Buddhism). This genealogical concern is typical of the Chinese social context in which the Chan school arose.

Paradoxically this doctrine that asserts that it is not a doctrine and situates itself outside of language has itself produced an enormous body of writing, occupying in length almost half of the Sino-Japanese canon. The literature is primarily composed of collections of propositions of Chan masters, essentially *koans* (Chinese: *gong'an*; literally "judicial cases used as precedents"), puzzles that cannot be solved by the intellect (since the intellect itself is the problem). The use of *koans* came to characterize the Rinzai school of Zen (Japanese for its founder, Linji,) while *zazen*, (sitting meditation) was held to be the characteristic of the Soto school. As it is

The bodhisattva Jizo. Engakuji, Kamakura, Japan. This bodhisattva, who was extremely popular in China and even more so in Japan, intercedes for souls after death, at the moment of supreme judgment. He guides them to the crossroads of the six pathways that lead to the next world (that is, rebirth in one of the six realms).

Koans.

Koans are enigmas such as "What is the sound of one hand clapping?" or "What was your original face before you were born?" Koans form the essential part of recorded dialogues such as the following between the master Linji Yixuan and one of his disciples: " While entering the meditation room, a monk asked: 'Of what is the sword blade made?' To which the master responded: 'Bad! Bad!' The monk hesitated, and the master struck him." Linji was famous for his use of force, often beating his disciples severely, providing some with the keys to enlightenment and others with bumps and bruises.

practiced by the latter, notably in Japan, *zazen* or *shikan taza* ("pure and simple seated posture") is not so much a form of introspection as a ritual imitation of the Buddha. Thus, it is not a matter of a method for reaching a goal (awakening), but of concretely manifesting an awakened state of mind that has already been reached.

Pure Land Buddhism

Buddhism of the Pure Land school developed around Buddha Amitabha (Japanese: Amida). Before entering into nirvana, this buddha was said to have taken numerous vows, notably that he would undertake to guide into his Pure Land in the West all who invoked his name with faith.

Amidism grew up in Japan simultaneously with the theory of the decline of the Law. According to a prophecy of the Buddha, five centuries after his *parinirvana*, the true Dharma would be supplanted by a counterfeit Law, itself followed a millennium later by the final Law (Japanese: *mappo*). When the world entered this final phase people would no longer be capable of understanding the truth of the Buddha's doctrine, much less practicing it. The Japanese of the twelfth century believed they had just entered this final period, and their belief seemed to be confirmed by disasters of all kinds

The Great Amida Buddha of Kamakura, Japan. Nearly 35 feet high, this statue was built in 1252. Like the Great Buddha of Todaiji in Nara, it was originally built inside a large hall. The hall burned down in 1495 and was never rebuilt.

Japanese sects.
The Chinese Pure Land school, which made its first appearance during the Tang dynasty, gave birth to many different sects in Japan: Jodushu, founded by Honen (d. 1212); Jodo Shinshu, founded by his disciple Shinran (d. 1262); and Jishu, founded by Ippen (1239-1289). Despite considerable differences all teach total abandonment to Amida and the invocation of his name, the *nenbutsu* (*Namu Amida Butsu*, "homage to the Buddha Amida").

Japanese monks performing a ceremony. Although some sects such as Chan/Zen are, in theory, rigorously anti-ritualistic, in practice Buddhism is a religion of ritual. Monastic life is ordered by liturgy and ritual.

that ravaged Japan at the time. In response, the founders of Amidism offered their very simple doctrine, which, they explained, was suited to the diminished capacities of people of these final days, who were incapable of putting into practice the teachings of the Buddha. Honen and Shinran preached the simple way, a way of salvation for all, made possible by the immense compassion of Buddha Amida.

Such absolute dependence on Amida led its followers to forsake the cult of all other Buddhas and a fortiori those of the *kamis*. This approach often verged on a kind of iconoclasm, which did not escape harsh criticism from the more traditional schools. To the extent that it called into question social structures that rested upon a synthesis of buddhas and *kamis* this sectarian tendency subjected the adherents of Pure Land — as well as those of the somewhat more radical school of Nichiren — to persecution by the central authority. Nichiren himself, whose diatribes spared no one, escaped execution only by a miracle and was sent into exile. Although he evinced little sympathy for Pure Land Buddhism, he seems to have been influenced by it nonetheless as he retained the practice of invoking the title of the *Lotus Sutra (daimoku)*, the sacred text of his school. Even though Nichiren's prophecies never came

Buddhist tricksters. Mahayana Buddhism has its share of colorful characters. These are the madmen of tantric or Chan Buddhism, whose eccentric behavior oversteps the bounds of Buddhist morality. But they represent a no less elevated conception of Buddhist truth. In Tibet, the best-known example was that of Dugpa Kunle; in China, the monks Hanshan and Shide are represented as comical and hairy figures. The Chan master Budai is a laughing incarnation of Maitreya. And in Japan the amorous exploits of the Zen master Ikkyu are the subject of many stories.

true, this text became one of the most popular in Japanese Buddhism.

Despite the doctrinal differences between Chan/Zen and the Pure Land school, both favored iconoclastic interpretations of Buddhist teaching, whereby traditional morality and pious deeds were disregarded in the name of a higher truth: the call of awakening or the certainty of Amida's grace. The case of the Nichiren sect is a bit special, since while it maintained that it was returning to original doctrines, its interpretation of the *Lotus Sutra* was idiosyncratic, and the implications of this were undoubtedly radical.

As a reaction, there were numerous attempts to reemphasize the importance of monastic discipline. There is a tendency to distinguish the new forms of Buddhism of the Kamakura period (Zen, Judo, Shinshu, Nichiren) from the older ones (Ritsu or Vinaya, Shingon, Tendai). In fact, reforms appeared in the Ritsu school as well as in Zen, which in turn was imbued with the Confucian ethic. In addition, the influence of esoteric Buddhism made itself felt in all of these sects: it is for this reason that the koans of Zen, like the *nenbutsu* of the Amidist sects, grew to resemble mantras, magic formulas used at funerals or to assure individual and collective prosperity. What was really new in the new religions was a sectarian spirit that was to contribute to the great religious revolutions of the sixteenth century.

Nichiren calligraphy. The Nichiren sect, one of the most influential in contemporary Japan, extols the talismanic properties of calligraphies representing the title of the Lotus Sutra, *their sacred text. According to Nichiren (d. 1282), this sutra contains the ultimate teaching of the Buddha, and recitation of its title* (daimoku) *guarantees liberation; all other practices are thought to be superfluous, even harmful.*

Jishu. Among the many Amidist schools, Jishu stands out because of its itinerant character. The monks specialize in giving aid to the dying, a quality much appreciated during war. When a Jishu priest receives the spiritual charge of a soldier, he follows him everywhere, so that he will be there at his last moments and can take charge of the funeral rites. Despite their vows of neutrality, these priests have sometimes abandoned their purely religious role to serve paramilitary functions. Although in many cases this entails merely seeking to preserve the life of a combatant. Despite criticisms, this school, whose leader was perceived to be a living Buddha, exerted considerable influence in Japan especially in the shogun period.

East Meets West

The story of the discovery of Buddhism by the West merits close examination, because it is a story of misunderstandings and prejudices, just the opposite of what one would expect from the rational approach of Western thought. The earliest accounts of Buddhism come from medieval explorers of the thirteenth century such as Marco Polo and Jean Du Plan Carpin, but they were not thought reliable. It was not until the missionary expansion of the sixteenth century that credible information was obtained regarding Chinese and Japanese religious practices. In 1549, a Jesuit missionary, Francis Xavier, arrived in Japan and described with a mixture of horror and admiration Japanese Buddhists, particularly Zen monks (among whom he made some friends).

The discovery of Buddhism in China had to wait a bit longer for Matteo Ricci and his successors. A few points ought to be noted.

To begin with, the Europeans who first encountered Buddhism had difficulty understanding and relating the two strands of thought they had encountered. This was perhaps because Buddhism had flourished in Japan but was in decline throughout China. More significantly, it was only much later that they realized that this religion was the same as the one that had long before flourished in India. The figure of the Buddha was not altogether unknown to the missionaries. He is even included, though somewhat

Opposite page: Meditation session at the Zen Mountain Monastery, Mt. Tremper, New York.

Below: Head of the Buddha, carved in rock. Longmen (the "Dragon's Gate") near Luoyang, China. This Chinese capital was the end point of the Silk Route during the Tang dynasty.

Jesuits in China.
The situation in which the Jesuits in China found themselves was rather strange, partly because Chinese officials often mistook them for Buddhist missionaries. Matteo Ricci quickly distinguished himself from his Buddhist rivals, whose reputations were often dubious. He turned instead to the ideas of Confucius.

Room of the 10,000 buddhas in the Shaolin Monastery, China. This is a meditation chamber, as one can see from the cushions on the floor. The same room is pictured on pages 87–88. At a time when the rhythms of modern life become more and more intrusive, many Westerners are attracted to the calm and simplicity of meditation, especially since it does not necessarily entail embracing specifically religious values.

surreptitiously, in the *Golden Legend* of Jacobus da Voragine, under the name of St. Josaphat.

Faced with disturbing similarities between Buddhist and Christian monasticism, the missionaries' reactions were ambivalent. On the one hand, they concluded that Buddhism had to be an offshoot of Nestorian Christianity transmitted to the Far East through Central Asia. The legend of St. Thomas, apostle of the Indies, contributed to this misapprehension. Wasn't the principal Buddhist apostle in China, named Damo (from Dharma, an abbreviation of Bodhidharma), said to have come out of the West? His name was quickly understood to be a mistranslation of Thomas (or Bartholomew). Ricci himself was a victim of this error. This thesis was abandoned with great reluctance; it could still find adherents at the beginning of our century.

In the meantime, another theory arose, according to which the similarities between Christianity and Buddhism could admit of only one solution: Buddha was the Antichrist, and his teaching was a parody of the true faith, destined to deceive overly credulous Orientals.

Most often, missionaries emphasized the differences between the two religions. The Buddhists for their part were active as well. In China and Japan, various refutations of Christianity were promulgated. After putting down a Christian revolt in 1634, the shogun government proscribed the Christian faith and used Buddhism as a vehicle for

Chan/Zen.
Chan Buddhism (better known by its Japanese name, Zen) teaches only one of many forms of Buddhist meditation. It is notable for its rejection of all forms of visualization and traditional imagery and for its insistence on the absence of thought. The goal is awakening, a state that the Zen master tries to induce in his pupils through the use of koans (enigmas that the intellect cannot solve) or shock treatment (blows, cries, insults).

ideological control. Laws were enacted that required all Japanese to be affiliated with a Buddhist temple. The close adherence of most Japanese families to Buddhism can be said to stem from the forced conversions of this era.

During the enlightenment of the eighteenth century, European scholars began seriously to study China of the Confucian period, wherein they found a model of enlightened despotism. Knowledge of this period derived from the edifying and curious letters of Jesuit missionaries, who were themselves influenced by Confucian thought. Consequently, Buddhism was not favorably reported. The situation would change in the nineteenth century, thanks to what contemporaries called, a bit prematurely, the oriental renaissance. This renaissance was marked by the rediscovery of India, which orientalists claimed was the cradle of all civilizations and the living source of mysticism. Although enthusiasm for India burned brightly during the first half of the century, Buddhism remained somewhat in shadow. But by the middle of the nineteenth century, the first Buddhist texts were being translated into European languages. For an era that had largely forgotten all the information gleaned by the missionaries in the preceding centuries, it seemed as if Buddhism were being discovered for the first time. This new generation assumed that the gross superstitions of

Western disciple with a Chan master in Italy. Buddhism has grown significantly in Europe and North America over the last few decades. Often it is pursued because of a super-ficial taste for the exotic rather than a real understanding of its traditions.

The monks and the philosophers.
European philosophers of the Enlightenment looked upon the Buddhist monastic tradition as just another form of clerical obscuantism. To them, monks were all rogues or idlers. Voltaire expressed the general sentiment: "Oh Buddhist monk/ since your goal is to deceive me/Try to do a little better at it."

Thanthog Rinpoche at Lama Ganchen, Milan. The fascination that Tibetan Buddhism exerts on the West is due in large measure to the presence of Tibetan exiles and the spiritual radiance of their leader, the Dalai Lama. It can also be explained by the aesthetic and symbolic character of Tibetan art and a doctrine that is at first glance sexually permissive. In reality this form of Buddhism constitutes only one small variant of the many forms of Buddhism practiced in Asia.

the Chinese Buddhists had nothing in common with the noble humanism of the Buddha himself. In fact, as a fuller understanding of Buddhist teaching began to emerge, it was found to be a powerful weapon for the forces of anticlericalism. On the other hand, this new taste for Buddhism was to produce trenchant counterattacks on the part of defenders of Western culture such as Barthélémy Saint-Hilaire.

Closer to our own time, Paul Claudel, whose work *Understanding the East* might better be entitled "Misunderstanding the East," could write in 1898 about Japan and its relationship with Buddhism: "These blind eyes refused to recognize unconditioned being, and it was given to the one they call the Buddha to perfect their pagan blasphemy." According to Claudel, "the Buddha found only nothingness, and his doctrine proposes a monstrous communion." He added, "For myself I find that they have added the idea of pleasure to that of nothingness. And this is the last Satanic mystery, the silence of the creature entrenched in its undivided refusal, the incestuous quietude of the soul centered on its essential uniqueness."

The lackluster orientalism of the nineteenth century gave way to the overenthusiastic orientalism of the beginning of the twentieth. Long vilified, Buddhism was now praised to the skies. In contrast to those like Saint-Hilaire who considered Buddhism a dangerous challenge to Western values, numerous admirers — including Schopenhauer and Nietzsche — found it a therapeutic antidote to Christianity. Their precursors were Thoreau and Emerson and the other American transcendentalists who saw in Buddhism (and Indian thought in general) an alternate pathway. *The Light of*

Freud and nirvana.
On the subject of nirvana Freud remarked rather astutely: "Nirvana is not nothingness, but the transcendence of all opposites. . . . Ah, you European dreamers! What do you know of the depths of oriental thought?"

Religion of reason.
Faced with diverse forms of neo-Buddhism steeped in the occultism of the Theosophical Society, a new modern Buddhism, purged of all cosmological, magical, and irrational elements, was proclaimed a "religion of reason." The

World Parliament of Religions held in Chicago in 1893, sought to make Hinduism and Buddhism (or at least certain aspects of them) known to the American public.

It was on this occasion that D. T. Suzuki, who was to become one of the most

Asia, a long poem on Buddhism by Sir Edwin Arnold, was reprinted one hundred times between 1879 and 1930.

Buddhism Today

Buddhism has varied according to the various Asian cultures in which it has flourished. We must confine ourselves here to sketching the broad outlines. In the face of growing nationalism, colonial expansion, and the combined assault of Western rationality and Christianity, Buddhism has been forced to undertake certain reforms. Sometimes these have come as result of certain internal pressures, as in Thailand, but more often they have been in reaction to outside threats. This was the case with the Meiji restoration in Japan (like most restorations, actually an ideological innovation), characterized by virulent anti-Buddhism. To restore its image Japanese Buddhism sought to dissociate itself from the superstitions of popular traditions. Rather it attempted to portray itself off as a philosophical system rich in ethical values and psychological insight. From this time dates Japanese interest in "original" Buddhism (that is, Indian Buddhism), to which the lion's share of Buddhist study has since been devoted.

As Max Weber has pointed out, insofar as it is a monastic system, Buddhism is characterized by a certain form of rationality. Some aspects of its philosophy can be easily harmonized with modern scientific theory; others, such as the cosmology it proposes, seem less compatible with Copernican theories of the universe. Concessions to

Kamakura Temple, Japan. Offerings for still-born or aborted infants. The bodhisattva Jizo presided over these devotions.

important interpreters of Mahayana thought (particularly Zen) in the West, began his work of popularization. For half a century, he was the preeminent conduit of Zen (presented a bit prematurely as the flower of oriental thought) and Japanese culture to the West. Others followed in his footsteps, and little by little Buddhism is acclimatizing itself to Western habits of thought.

Child at Todaiji, Nara, Japan. Incense burners, which are found in most Buddhist holy places, are legacies of China. Along with icons, they are important foci of religious activity in the temple.

science have been made, but sometimes at the expense of fundamental principles.

In adapting to the modern world, Buddhism has had to redefine its social and political roles as well. Historically, the Buddhist clergy has been closely linked to the ruling powers and has helped to legitimize feudal and monarchical power. With the adoption of political systems established (in theory) along democratic lines, Buddhism has found itself more actively engaged in social causes. In India, it has made a comeback, becoming a mass movement due to efforts of Doctor Ambedkar (d. 1956), who struggled for the emancipation of the untouchables.

The other significant aspect of Buddhism's evolution in this century has been its introduction in the West. European critiques stemmed not only from the needs of the Christian cause in Asia, but also from the strong appeal Buddhist ideas held for Western intellectual elites from early on. The labors of D. T. Suzuki, notably his *Essays on Zen Buddhism* (1927), popularized this form of Japanese Buddhism. The 1950s witnessed a flourishing of writings on Zen, with the works of Richard H. Blyth on Zen and its impact on Western literature, the explorations of Eastern philosophy by Alan Watts (*The Way of Zen*, 1959), and particularly with its celebration by Beat poets and writers such as Jack Kerouac (*Dharma Bums*, 1958), Allen Ginsberg, and Gary Snyder. This led to an

Zen in the West.
Since the 1960s, Western culture has transformed Zen into an entity practically independent of Buddhism. Some consider this a strange phenomenon and see a certain degradation occurring. Certainly it is somewhat of an oversimplification.

To take root in Western societies Buddhism must adapt itself, and there is always the danger that this will be perceived as a deterioration.

explosion of interest with the so-called counter-culture of the sixties and the New Age that followed. Enough indications of widespread interest exist to suggest that Buddhism has become more than a passing fad.

No doubt the dangers of popularization are real, but the possibilities of expansion are as great if not greater. There is no doubting the sincerity of representatives such as the Vietnamese monk Thich Nhat Hanh or the Dalai Lama, who are willing to take up the challenges of modern life in order to preserve the benefits of traditional ways. Whereas Buddhism has won a wide audience among an occidental public that is largely Protestant, contemplative and cosmopolitan, Asian immigration since the end of the last century — principally in North America — has had important social consequences and led to the emergence of ethnic forms of Buddhism in the West. If these have not yet had a great impact on the immigrants' new homelands, nor on the intellectuals who traditionally have been drawn to Buddhist ideas, their importance is bound to increase.

Monks begging in Kyoto, Japan, in a striking contrast of modernity and tradition.

Electronic canon. The availability of the Pali, and soon the Sino-Japanese, canon in an electronic edition should stimulate research and lead to a better understanding of Buddhism.

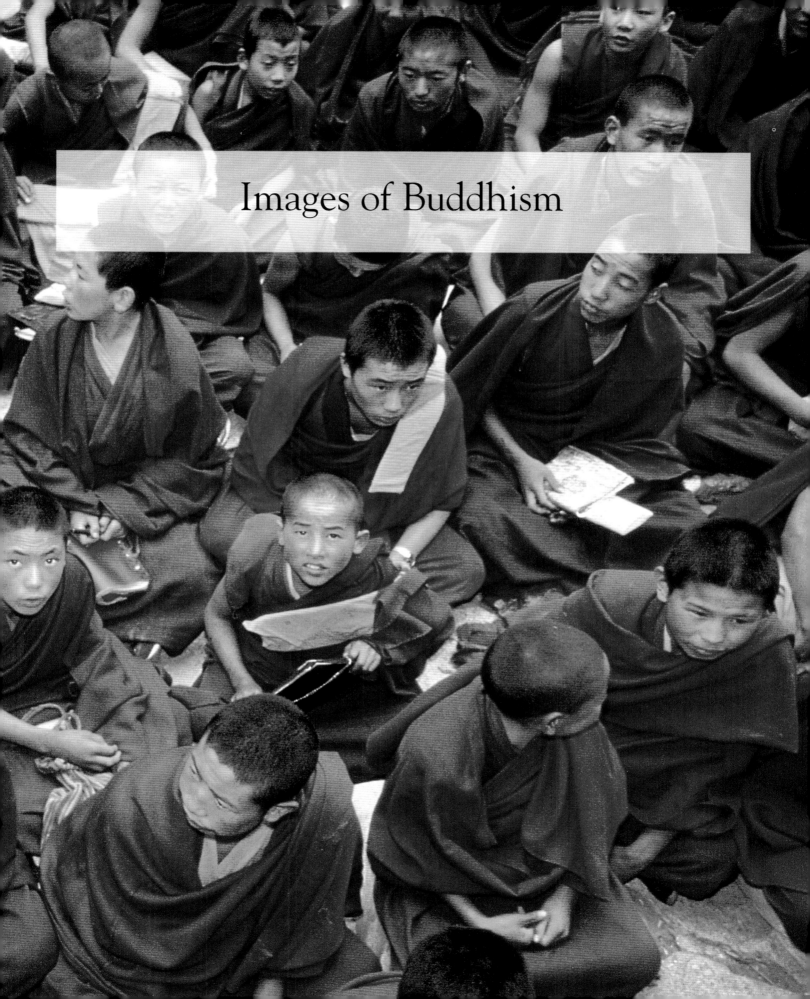

Images of Buddhism

Preceding spread: *Novices with their prayer books. Drepung Monastery, Tibet.*

Veneration of the Buddha. Cave 10, Ajanta, India. In the gesture of veneration, the palms of the hands are pressed together.

Opposite page: *Bodhisattva in meditation. Cave 17, Ajanta, India. Ajanta is one of the most spectacular places in India. Over 20 temples decorated with sculptures and frescoes of astonishing colors in the pure (Gupta) style of Buddhist Indian art illustrate the principles of the Mahayana tradition.*

Monastery in ruins with stupas, India. The isolation of Buddhist monasteries stems from a mode of thought that asserts the primacy of the spiritual over the worldly life. In the early days, Buddhist monks retired into solitude to devote themselves to meditation and study, the path that led to enlightenment.

The Buddha in parinirvana *(final nirvana) with his disciple Ananda. Group of statues, 12th century, Polannaruwa, Sri Lanka.*

Opposite page: *Detail.*

The Great Buddha in meditation. Gal Vihara Temple, 12th century, Polannaruwa, Sri Lanka. A nun makes an offering (puja) *to the Buddha.*

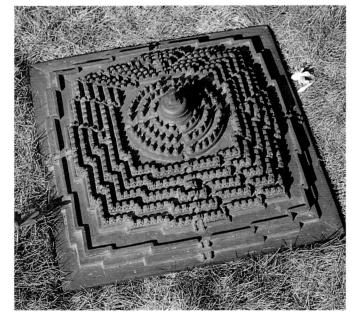

Above: *Bas-relief representing the Buddha. Borobudur, Indonesia. Borobudur, a Buddhist monument of the ninth century in the center of Java, ranks as one of the world's greatest architectural achievements. A mountain temple in the form of a mandala, decorated with statuary and scenes in bas-relief, it is also an ancient meditation site.*

At right: *A model of Borobudur.*

Opposite page: *Borobudur. Upper terrace of pyramid, with five terraces with buddhas housed in latticed stupas (with the exception of the statue of the Buddha in the foreground).*

Angkor Thom (600–1100), Cambodia (Kampuchea). Angkor Thom is a monument constructed by the "divine king" of the Khmer dynasty, Jayavarman, in honor of the Lord of the Worlds, Lokeshvara. Here one sees one of the gates to the inner court of the temple. The highest tower represents Mount Sumeru, the cosmic axis that supports the three levels: hell, earth, and the celestial regions.

Below: Angkor Wat, Cambodia.

Opposite page: Bas-relief, Angkor Thom. The bas-relief of Angkor Thom, like those in Pagan in Burma or Borobudur in Indonesia immortalize in stone the entire mythological and metaphysical world view of Indian Buddhism. These monuments constitute a kind of book in stone from which the faithful can decipher their entire sacred history. Unfortunately, this history is legible today only to some archaeologists and art historians.

Pagan, Burma. The construction of Pagan lasted for over two centuries (900–1100). Exemplifying the Burmese and Mon styles, it consists of over 5,000 buildings that remain in very good condition.

Shwethalyaung Buddha.
Paya, Rangoon (Yangon),
Burma.

Opposite page:
Shwethalyaung Buddha, Bago
(Pegu), Burma.

Following spread:
Pagoda of Shwe Dagon,
Rangoon, Burma
(1300–1400). This pagoda
is one of the most richly
decorated constructions in
Southeast Asia.

Monk performing a ritual.
Bangkok, Thailand.

Opposite page: *Krabi,*
Thailand.

Buddhism is the state religion
of Thailand. All schoolchildren
take classes in monasteries to
experience the contemplative
life even thought they may
later choose to engage in
worldly pursuits. The sight of
hundreds of monks going
about their business each
morning through the streets of
Bangkok illustrates the vitality
of Buddhism in Thai society.
Buddhist art in Thailand with
its multiplicity of gilded icons, is
a sign of Buddhism's
omnipresence.

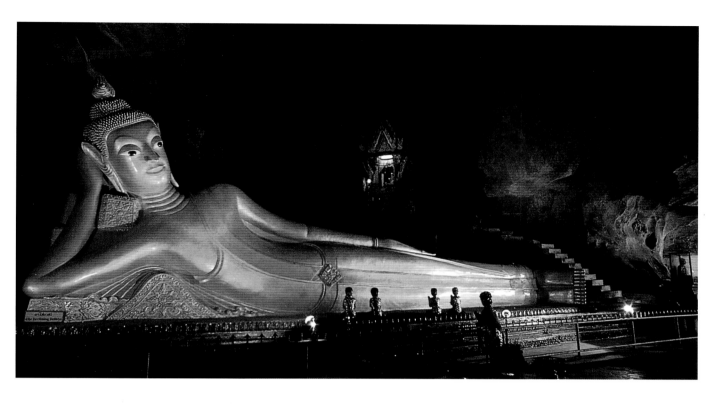

Potala Palace, Lhasa, Tibet.
The monastery fortress of
Potala is named after Potalaka,
the paradise of bodhisattva,
Avalokiteshvara. It was built by
the fifth Dalai Lama as a
statement of his power. Today,
under Chinese domination, it is
a state museum.

Yungang, China. The caves of Yungang protect immense buddhas carved in rock and narrative bas-reliefs. These are primarily the work of an emperor of the first Wei dynasty (ca. 460 AD) as a response to the persecutions visited on Buddhists in the 20 years preceding his reign.

Following spread: *Interior of a cave, Yungang.*

Buddhist ceremony at Shaolin Monastery, during which the sutras are recited. Shaolin Monastery, the birthplace of the Chan/Zen school, was recently rebuilt by the Chinese government. It was there that the patriarch Bodhidharma established himself in the sixth century. The monastery was strategically located near the onetime capital of China (Luoyang) and consequently was exposed to frequent attacks. As a result, the monks developed the martial arts techniques that are widely practiced today. For this reason, Bodhidharma is considered the patron of kung-fu (literally "technique") and shorinji kempo (Shaolin boxing). At present, there seems to be renewed interest in Buddhism in China, and Shaolin Monastery has become a pilgrimage site as well as a tourist attraction.

Monks in prayer. Chiang Mai, Thailand.

Below: *Ceremony in the Jinshan temple, China.*

Above: *Ceremony commemorating the 1,200th anniversary of the establishment of the great Tendai monastery, Enryakuji, on Mount Hiei near Kyoto. The Tendai school was founded by the monk Saicho in reaction to the worldly Buddhism of Nara. It derives from the Chinese Tiantai school.*

Below: *Ceremony at the Jokhang Temple, Tibet. The Jokhang is one of the oldest and holiest monasteries in all of Tibet.*

Following spread: *Hall of the Great Buddha, Todaiji, Nara, Japan. Built with funds raised by Gyoki, it is representative of the popular traditions of Buddhism.*

Vairocana, the Great Buddha of Todaiji, Nara, Japan. Forty-five feet high. Vairocana's imposing stature represents centralized power in the Nara era, personified in the emperor, the Buddha's counterpart on earth.

Opposite page: *Nyoirin Kannon. Todaiji, Nara, Japan.*

Above: *The bodhisattva Jizo (Kshitigarbha). Todaiji, Nara, Japan.*

Above: Zazen *hall (Zen sitting meditation). One should practice zazen in calm surroundings, seated in the lotus position with the eyes half-open.*

Below: *Zen calligraphy of Suzuki Sochu Roshi. Nojiri Michiko collection, Rome.*

Opposite page: *Zen rock garden. Taizo-in, Kyoto.*

Rituals and Practice

Historical questions aside, the Buddha rapidly became a legendary and then a divine figure. In the process, he had to coexist with other purely metaphysical buddhas, who at times surpassed his popularity. In the earliest Buddhist texts, the Buddha is already called *devatideva*, god beyond gods. His legend seems to have expanded as stories of his past lives began to be told. The most popular of these tales describe the Buddha's extraordinary altruism. A characteristic example tells the story of his earlier existence as Prince Vessantara. The generosity of this prince knew no bounds. He not only disposed of his riches but of his wife and children as well, who were sold into slavery. The scandalous flavor of the story was mitigated in some versions by a happy ending in which the bodhisattva is reunited with his loved ones. It is made clear that this was a test imposed by the gods, which the hero passed with flying colors.

Along with the proliferation of these legendary stories, debates arose as to whether the Buddha was a corporeal or a supernatural being. Although Mahayana Buddhism has a tendency to emphasize the human traits of Buddhist saints, in the *Lotus Sutra*, one of its most important texts, the Buddha is revealed as a supernatural being. This sutra has had a tremendous influence; in it the Buddha reveals to his followers assembled around him on Vulture Peak Mountain that his existence transcends life and death. In the face of their disbelief, he calls forth the innumerable disciples to whom he has taught the dharma since the dawn of time. And, as if that were not enough, he causes another buddha, Prabhutaratna, to appear, seated in meditation in a stupa that floats in midair. The miraculous atmosphere that suffuses this sutra is characteristic of Mahayana texts. Following another tradition, the Buddha's death comes to resemble the sacrifice of primordial man, a motif common to many mythological

Devatideva.
According to legend, the name *devatideva* was given to the Buddha by his father, Shuddhodhana. One day, he brought his son to the ancestral temple to pay his respects to the clan gods: miraculously, the statues prostrated to the young prince.

traditions. It is said that he abandoned a third of his longevity for the benefit of future generations.

The earliest representations of the Buddha were all symbolic. Perhaps out of reverence for his transcendental nature, his followers hesitated to portray his likeness. Rather his presence was conveyed by icons such as the Bodhi tree or the Wheel of Dharma. Another important symbol was his footprints. These can be found imprinted in rocks throughout Asia, even as far off as Japan. The aniconism of early Buddhism at last gave way to anthropomorphic representations. Questions regarding how this important stylistic change occurred still occupy scholars. Still, this Buddha, divine being that he is, is just the Buddha of our cosmic age, one in a line of eight. The existence of past buddhas seem to have been devised to account for the Buddha's apprenticeship, which was said to have

lasted through innumerable rebirths. How else could he have hit upon the idea of enlightenment, if he himself had not been taught by another Buddha? Thus legend has it that he was once the disciple of the buddha Dipankara, who foretold his apotheosis. Dipankara was but one of Shakyamuni's seven predecessors. The Buddha also is destined to be succeeded in the distant future by a final buddha, Maitreya. In multiplying the number of buddhas and the universes over which they preside, the Mahayana tradition broke out of the linear and eschatological conventions of earlier teachings. Buddhas could now manifest in all times and all places. The world had become the arena for a vast game of hide-and-seek, in which seekers could hope to encounter their ideal.

The most important of these atemporal and potentially omnipresent buddhas — those who were not too abstract to become

objects of popular veneration — were Amida, buddha of the Pure Land, and Yakushi, the healing buddha. But the place of honor, according to the tantric tradition, is given to Vairocana (Japanese: Dainichi), of whom all other buddhas are simply manifestations.

Buddha Dainichi (Vairocana). Great stupa on Mount Koya in Japan. In the Shingon school, the object of the highest veneration is not the Buddha Shakyamuni, but the cosmic buddha Vairocana. According to Shingon teachings, the entire universe is nothing other than the body of the cosmic Buddha.

Below: *A Greco-Indian Buddha of Gandhara. Mathura Museum, India.*

Footprints of the Buddha.
The most famous set of footprints are found in Sri Lanka. Marco Polo described them as Adam's footprints in paradise (which tradition placed in Sri Lanka.).

Anthropomorphism.
The traditional theory is that the first anthropomorphic representations of the Buddha were the product of a Greco-Indian tradition that flourished in the Gandhara region (present-day Afghanistan) after the conquests of

Alexander. The orientalist connotations of this thesis have been challenged by recent scholarship.

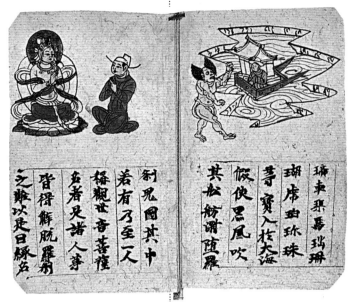

Page from the Lotus Sutra *found at Dunhuang. British Library, London. Salvation is promised to all who recite or copy this sutra. This manuscript was one of many discovered in a grotto in Dunhuang.*

Below: *The Chinese pilgrim and translator Xuanzang (seventh century). Ninth century painting from Dunhuang. British Museum, London.*

After the Buddha's final nirvana, his disciples gathered in a series of councils to rule on disputes concerning the interpretation of his doctrine. The responsibility for the oral preservation of his teachings was entrusted to various groups. Thus oral transmission formed the basis for the canon; it was not until the beginning of the common era, some four centuries later, that these works were written down in the Pali language in Sri Lanka. There is no question that by that time the teachings had undergone a considerable evolution. Thus, the relationship between the Pali canon and the Buddha's original doctrine remains problematic.

For many centuries the teachings of Buddhism were confined to the oral tradition in India, but it was as written texts that they spread throughout the rest of Asia. In China particularly, where writing was endowed with a quasi-magical potency, the progressive discovery of a vast corpus of Buddhist texts guaranteed that the intellectual elites would be favorably disposed to the new religion. These sacred writings were held to be of such value that Chinese (and later Japanese) pilgrims often risked their lives to locate them. At the beginning of this century, a major trove of Buddhist writings in Chinese, Tibetan and other Central Asian languages was discovered in a grotto in the Dunhuang oasis, one of the principal stops on the Silk Route. Many of these manuscripts were brought back to Europe by Sir Aurel Stein and Paul Pelliot.

According to tradition, the Buddhist canon was established in oral form at the Council of Rajagriha (the capital of Magadha, in the Ganges River valley) shortly after the Buddha's *parinirvana*, but it is known to us only through later recensions in Pali and Sanskrit. The Pali texts have been regarded as those closest to the earliest teachings. This perception guided the work of the first translations into European languages, which were done in the nineteenth century under the auspices of the Pali Text Society. But the Pali canon includes texts from only one of the major schools of Buddhism, the others having disappeared from India by the time the work of transcription began.

In their various recensions the Pali texts are divided into three parts known as the Tripitaka ("Three Baskets"): the sutras, discourses of the Buddha; the Vinaya, texts pertaining to the conduct of monastic life; and the

Xuanzang. The most famous Buddhist pilgrim to research Buddhist scripture was Xuanzang (d. 664). He was also one of its most important translators. His pilgrimage to India formed the basis of the 17th century mythological novel *A Voyage to the West*. It was by posing as a follower of Xuanzang that Sir Aurel Stein persuaded the Taoist priest who had discovered the trove of manuscripts at Dunhuang to part with a substantial number of them. His price was a loaf of bread.

Abhidharma, scholarly texts that interpret the Buddha's teaching (*shastras*). Each sutra opens with the formula: "Thus have I heard." They are attributed to the Buddha's close disciple, Ananda, renowned for his prodigious memory. He was entrusted with the task of reciting the words of the master. In reality, all of the texts come from a much later time.

The Sanskrit canon is generally considered to be more inclusive, since it contains Mahayana texts not found in the Pali canon. One series of important Mahayana texts addresses the Perfection of Wisdom (*Prajnaparamita*). The most celebrated are the *Diamond Sutra* (*Vajracchedika-sutra*) and the *Heart Sutra* (*Hridaya-sutra*). These Mahayana texts are supposedly transcriptions of sermons that took place in more or less mythical places such as the Vulture Mountain Peak. The tantras are still later texts. They form the basis of tantric Buddhism. These are set in wholly mythological places, for example, in the vagina (*bhaga*) of a female deity, signifying the energy of the Buddha, from which derives the title of one such work, *Bhagavat* (Happiness).

After an intense effort that lasted from the fourth through the seventh century C.E., the Chinese canon, which was to become the basis of those of Korea and Japan, finally reached its definitive form. Later modifications consisted principally of the exclusion of some "apocryphal" texts.

The Tibetan canon was constituted through a unique set of circumstances. After the conversion of Tibet to Buddhism in the eighth century, Tibetan writing was invented with the sole aim of translating Buddhist texts from Sanskrit. Hence, written Tibetan is ideally suited to convey the nuances of Buddhist thought. The

Monk reading a sacred text, Shyangboche Monastery, Nepal. The reading of scripture is, as in most religions, a basic part of Buddhist practice.

At left: *The Buddha's first sermon, illustration from the* Heart Sutra. *Tibetan painting. Museum of Oriental Art, Rome.*

The Lotus Sutra.
This text has enjoyed immense prestige in both China and Japan over centuries. Its contents are, however, of a largely polemical character: it is, among other things, a criticism of the rules of the Hinayana school.

The Heart Sutra.
It is possible that this sutra was compiled in China, not in India as generally thought. It is a breviary in an extremely condensed form on the concept of *shunyata* (the emptiness of phenomena).

Tantra.
The two most influential tantric texts are the *Guhyasamaja* (*Secret Assembly*) and the *Mahavairocana-sutra* (*Sutra of the Cosmic Buddha, Vairocana*).

Below: Sutra of the Final Nirvana (Mahaparinirvana-sutra). *Copy dating from the Northern Wei dynasty, Dunhuang, China.*

At right: *Entry into the Jokhang Temple. Procession of praying monks. Lhasa, Tibet.*

translations into Tibetan remain so close to the Sanskrit originals that in some cases fragmentary Sanskrit texts were reconstructed by referring to the Tibetan versions. There are two parts to the Tibetan canon: the Tengyur

(sutras) and the Kangyur (doctrinal treatises). In addition, periodically over the centuries certain "treasures" (terma) have been recovered. These are texts that Tibetan Buddhists believe were hidden by the buddha Padmasambhava when Buddhism first took root in Tibet. Quite recently another "treasure" has come to light, renewing Tibetans' connection to ancient Buddhist practices in spite of the Chinese occupation.

Some have attributed the origins of Mahayana Buddhism to the development of a cult of stupas, others to a cult of texts. The major role played by the *Lotus Sutra* as a cult object is beyond question. The sutra promises that all those who recite or copy it will achieve enlightenment. At the same time, numerous stories of the miraculous powers of this sutra and others circulated widely. The content of the texts was of little importance.

"Apocryphal" texts. The criteria of authenticity for Buddhism are simple but somewhat problematic. In India, the term "apocryphal" was reserved for those texts that seemed not to have been preached by the Buddha. In China, the term distinguished texts that had been compiled in China, those that had been translated from Sanskrit.

The abstruse commentaries of the Abhidharma, for example, are sung in the rituals of Buddhism popularly practiced throughout Thailand. This mantric or incantatory function is found even with a text as philosophical as the *Heart Sutra*, a condensation of the *Perfection of Wisdom Sutra*. In China, certain adepts used their own blood to copy the sutras in hopes of accumulating merit to assure them favorable rebirths or benefits in their current lifetimes. Copying the sutras, even in plain ink, turned out to be a major enterprise, requiring the mobilization of vast numbers of scribes and artists. Magnificent illuminated manuscripts still exist, such as a copy of the *Lotus Sutra* in which each character rests upon a minuscule lotus. In Japan, the influence of the fine arts gave birth to copies wherein one finds illustrations from the classic novel *Genji Monogatari*. Many texts were written in gold letters on a blue background. One of the most beautiful examples is attributed to the hand of Taira no Kiyomori, a Japanese warlord of the twelfth century.

A non-canonical Buddhism exists as well. In a sense, the use of texts as cult objects rather than for didactic or philosophical purposes already stretches the boundaries of the notion of a canon. But more important was the flowering of apocryphal stories, especially in China. The requirements for inclusion in the canon varied widely in different times and places. When the Mahayana canon was definitively fixed during the Tang dynasty, all texts that were proved not to have originated in India, and therefore could not be attributed to the Buddha himself, were relegated to apocryphal status. At the same time, the talismanic character of Buddhist scripture was preserved by recourse to the ingenious concept of the revolving canon. This idea parallels on a grander scale the Tibetan prayer wheel. The revolving canon is a large wheel that contains all of the Buddhist canonical writings. By making it turn one complete revolution the aspirant is said to acquire the merit earned by reading or reciting the canon in its entirety.

Library of the Potala Palace, Lhasa, Tibet. The library contains the Tibetan Buddhist canon, a faithful translation of the Sanskrit originals.

The Platform Sutra.
A particularly significant example of an extra-canonical text in China is the *Platform Sutra of the Sixth Patriarch*, a fundamental text of Chan Buddhism attributed to the patriarch Huineng (d. 713). Despite this school's insistence that it was founded on a special transmission outside of scripture and that it did not rely on the written word, this text was venerated as a cult object whose possession was sufficient to guarantee the orthodoxy of an adept. Calling this work a sutra — a term reserved at that time for the words of the Buddha — shows that this school considered the patriarch worthy of designation as a buddha, even though he was not Indian, or even Chinese. (It appears he was a member of an ethnic minority.)

Buddhist Cosmology

Tibetan mandala (detail). The buddha at the center is surrounded at the four cardinal points by divinities. A mandala (literally "magic circle") offers practitioners a synthetic image of the Buddhist pantheon. It functions to capture and contain all the energies of the universe.

For a long time, Buddhism has been seen as an essentially cosmological doctrine. If, as tradition informs us, the Buddha refused to speculate on whether or not the world is eternal, his disciples did not hesitate to address such questions. Cosmology soon became an essential element in Buddhist teaching. The Buddhism that was adopted by Chinese and Japanese converts was not so much a moral or religious system, as a quasi-scientific way of approaching the world. In its broad outlines, the Buddhist vision was that of Hinduism. Certainly, there were radical departures in certain specific regards, but as Buddhism spread to a wider audience, it tended to revert to the reference points of traditional cosmology.

At the same time, Buddhism can be seen as an attempt to leave the cosmos behind. As Paul Mus has observed, Buddhist cosmology exists only to be transcended. The world is like a burning house, a dangerous place that it is best to leave as quickly as possible. The universe is only a stage set on which the drama of liberation is played out. Transmigration through the six realms does not provide fulfillment. Since the beginning of time, each individual has occupied all positions in the hierarchy of beings; the only worthwhile goal is to transcend *samsara* entirely.

Although Buddhism in its first stages has been described as without cosmology, in fact, Buddhist cosmology developed quite early on. One can distinguish two cosmological systems: the first holds there is only one world, the second that there are multiple worlds.

The one-world system is the more generally accepted system, found in the Hinayana and Mahayana traditions. The multiple-world system is expounded in certain Mahayana texts.

According to the one-world system, the center of the world is Mount Sumeru, which functions as a kind of column supporting the three levels of the universe: hell, the human world, and the dwelling places of celestial beings. The world is a flat disk with the sky and spheres of meditation above and hell below. It rests upon four supports, or wheels, those of earth, water, wind, and space. Mount Sumeru is surrounded by five concentric circles of

One-world system . In the system of a single world, three spheres are demarcated: that of desire, of subtle energies, and of immateriality. According to this system, various degrees of spiritual attainment correspond to these three levels. While ordinary humans, transmigrating through the six realms of *samsara*, remain captive in the sphere of desire, the Buddhist aspirant can escape through meditation. The first four degrees of *dhyana* correspond to the world of subtle energies, the final four to immateriality.

One's level of attainment in meditation determines the world of one's rebirth.

oceans, each ring separated by a band of mountains. Beyond the outermost ocean, there are four continents situated at the four cardinal points. Our homeland, Jambudvipa, lies to the south. The other three continents also have human inhabitants, but their size and life spans are different from ours. At the summit of Mount Sumeru, Indra, a vedic god, rules over the Heaven of the Thirty-three Gods.

Certain Mahayana texts present another cosmological system, in which a multitude — perhaps even an infinitude — of worlds, or buddha fields, coexist. Some of these are pure, others impure, and still others mixed. The world we live in, called Saha, is impure; it is the field of the Buddha Shakyamuni and is situated in the south. This meridional orientation is hard to fit into an infinite cosmos, consisting, in theory, of three thousand large universes, each of which comprises an infinite number of smaller universes such as our own. The life spans of the inhabitants of

these universes can vary greatly, lasting from ten years to eighty thousand.

With an infinite number of universes and a proliferation of buddhas, the notion of time is dwarfed by that of space. Time seems to be swallowed up in a black hole. Buddhas are everywhere, "as numerous as grains of sand on the shores of the Ganges." According to this conception, liberation becomes a cosmic drama. It is no longer a case of an individual attaining nirvana (as in the one-world system), but of a cosmic buddha who puts into play unimaginably vast energies over inconceivable stretches of time. Nirvana for the cosmic buddha means the liberation of all created beings, since they are nothing other than the buddha himself.

These two cosmological visions, then, offer radically different notions of liberation. In the first case, liberation is a slow, arduous process; in the second, buddhas and bodhisattvas (and sometimes practitioners as well) can travel to other worlds, such

as the Pure Land of Buddha Amitabha, at the speed of light.

For the most part, however, the system of a single world and its symbolism of the center dominated Buddhist imagery and cosmological speculation.

Mandala. Tibetan tangka, 18th century.

Yama, king of the underworld. Taimadera, Nara, Japan. Of Indian origin, Yama is one of ten kings of the underworld in popular Chinese mythology. But in Japanese mythology, he is invested with supreme authority. He is the impartial judge of the dead.

The cosmic mountain. Mount Sumeru plays an important role in the symbolism and architecture of Buddhism. The Buddhist stupa is perceived as a replica of this cosmic mountain. It is also a mandala, a sacred space, in which Buddha Vairocana,

the cosmic buddha, sits upon the lotus. The aspirant guides his steps toward this center (physically or through spiritual practices), finally identifying himself with the Buddha. The symbolism of the lotus is thus grafted onto that of the cosmic

mountain. Its petals represent the eight points of the compass and signify transcendence of the physical world.

Dancers in Kasuga Taisha, Nara, Japan. In earlier times, Japanese Buddhism coexisted with indigenous local cults. The principal Buddhist holy days sometimes have purely local resonances. Kamis and Buddhist saints can be honored together in the same ceremonies, bringing together Buddhist and Shinto priests (sometimes one and the same person). The rites of the Buddhist monastery Kofukuji in Nara, for example, are closely associated with the ceremonies held at the Shinto sanctuary of Kasuga.

The infant Buddha. Dunhuang, China. The white elephant appeared in a dream to the Buddha's mother, Maya, the night of his immaculate conception.

Like those of other religions, Buddhist celebrations are observed according to a liturgical calendar. The principal holy days relate to Buddhist history and commemorate important events in the life of the Buddha. The most widely observed are the anniversaries of his birth, enlightenment, and entry into final nirvana. The Buddha's birthday (Japanese: *kanbutsu-e*), celebrated in the ancient lunar calendar on the eighth day of the fourth month, is now observed on April 8. During the ceremonies priests intone prayers for children. The principal ritual consists of bathing a statue of the infant Buddha. The bath is drawn with a decoction of chrysanthemum leaves, which are known for their curative powers.

The anniversary of the Buddha's enlightenment (Japanese: *jodo-e*) is celebrated on December 8. It honors Shakyamuni's asceticism and the forty-nine days he spent under the Bodhi tree prior to his awakening. In Zen monasteries, this date marks the end of a particularly intense period of retreat and meditation, the *rohatsu sesshin* (December 1 to 8).

The anniversary of the Buddha's *parinirvana* was observed on the fifteenth day of the second month of the lunar calendar. It is now variously celebrated either on February 15 or March 15. The ceremonies center upon an image of the Buddha, sometimes represented by a very large statue, lying down in a grove of trees near Kushinagara. He is shown on the verge of entering nirvana surrounded by his tearful disciples and groups of animals.

There are many festivals in the first lunar month, since it is thought to contain the seeds of an entire year. Since Asia uses two calendars these holy days are often duplicated. New Year celebrations can be held on January 1 and in February–March when the year begins according to the lunar calendar.

Buddhist celebrations for the New Year in China and Japan are integrated with underlying folk traditions in a complex fashion. The festival culminates as a bell is struck eight hundred times signaling the beginning of the new year. In contrast to the practice in China and Vietnam, the lunar new year in Japan is not celebrated as such. However, the Japanese do celebrate a holiday called *setsubun* ("separation of the seasons"), which coincides with the Chinese New Year. It is at such times of cosmic renewal that danger can threaten and therefore must be vigilantly guarded against. Rites of exorcism that take place during *setsubun* have become extremely popular. Householders throw handfuls of beans — whose magical properties are widely recognized in Asia — across the thresholds of their homes while crying: "Demons, away; good spirits, enter!" During the festival, certain temples enact a pantomime in which the priest chases his

Other holidays.
Along with holidays marking significant events in the Buddha's life are those that commemorate the anniversaries of the deaths of the founders and patriarchs of particular sects. Zen monasteries celebrate the anniversary of

the death of Bodhidharma, the legendary monk who is credited with bringing the Chan/Zen doctrine from India to China. Sometimes there are holidays on particularly significant days such as the 700th year anniversary of the death of the founder of

Shinshu (the Pure Land school), which was celebrated in 1962. And, of course, each monastery celebrates the anniversary of its founder.

acolytes, who are disguised as demons (*oni*), before exorcising the crowd of the faithful.

Another important Buddhist festival in Japan is *higan* (literally, "the other shore"). This holiday is celebrated twice a year, at the vernal and autumnal equinoxes. It lasts for a week during which sutras are read continually in the temples and families visit cemeteries to pay homage to the dead. "The other shore" signifies for Buddhists the goal of all of their efforts: liberation, or nirvana. *Higan* is a translation of the Sanskrit *paramita*, the cardinal virtue of the bodhisattvas. The equinoxes, points of equilibrium between day and night, are apt cosmological symbols for the Buddha's teaching of the Middle Way, the path between the clarity of wisdom and the darkness of ignorance. *Higan* is also a harvest festival, uniting the cult of the sun with the cult of ancestors.

Another major holiday, which played an important role in the acceptance and spread of Buddhism in China and Japan, is *Ullambana* (Chinese: *Yulanpen*; Japanese: *Urabon* or more commonly *Obon*). This festival is also called the Day of Universal Deliverance (Chinese: *Pudu*) and is equivalent to All Saints' Day in the West. Traditionally, it fell on the fifteenth day of the seventh lunar month; today it is celebrated from July 13–16. During this time, ancestors as well as family ghosts (who have not yet attained the status of ancestors) come back to earth to visit the living. The returning spirits are treated as honored guests; banquets with dancing are held in their honor. On the night of July 15, scraps of paper and bamboo are lit and then set to float upon the water to guide the spirits back to their abode in the underworld. In Kyoto, the hills surrounding the city are lit with thousands of lights that form different symbols and signposts to guide the spirits of the dead home.

Ceremony in observance of the birthday of the Buddha. Seoul, South Korea. The major festivals mark the important dates of the Buddha's life: his birth, awakening, and parinirvana.

The legend of Mulian. It was in seventh century China that the holiday *Pudu* (Day of Universal Deliverance) developed in honor of Mulian, one of the Buddha's disciples. Despite his supernormal powers, which allowed him to find his mother in the underworld, he had to confess that he was unable to accomplish her liberation. On the advice of the Buddha, he made offerings to all of the buddhas, past, present, and future, that they would enable him to save his mother and all suffering beings. The legend of Mulian had considerable impact in a society where filial piety and the cult of ancestors played such a predominant role.

The Buddha along with bodhisattvas and other deities. Tibetan painting, Maraini collection, Florence.

Below: *Jizo with the judges of the underworld. Uzuki, Japan. The Buddhist conception of hell is more along the lines of purgatory, since those condemned to dwell there will in time be reborn in another realm.*

Buddhism preaches the impermanence of all things and the omnipresence of death. In each moment, death visits us sixteen times; each breath could be our last. And according to Buddhist funerary rituals death, is a long process that begins well before — and, more importantly, continues well after — one steps over its threshold, and crosses "the shallow stream." The paradox of transmigration without a persisting self that transmigrates is experienced as a purely doctrinal one and does not seem to cause problems in practice. Funerary rites designed to help guide the soul from one life to another last for forty-nine days, during which the spirit of the deceased wanders in an intermediate state between two worlds (the *bardo* state described in the *Tibetan Book of the Dead*). According to Chinese belief, it is during this time that the soul is ushered into judgment before a tribunal headed by Yama, the king of the underworld. The judges determine the conditions of the soul's next rebirth based upon its conduct in its previous life. The elaborate conception of the afterlife that Buddhism offers is one reason for its great popularity throughout the Far East. In early Buddhism, the rewards and punishments for one's actions were the result of an almost automatic process affecting one's present life and future births as well.

Whether determined by impersonal (karmic) law or the judgment of Yama, rebirth marks the end of the intermediate period. The returning being is reborn into one of the six destinies that constitute the world of desire, *samsara*. Those who have led the worst lives find themselves in one of the eighteen infernal regions. But all things come to an end, even the lowest rebirth. Thus, for Buddhists, hell is more akin to the Christian notion of purgatory. Eventually the damned will be reborn to a higher level in the hierarchy of destinies. The second level is that of the hungry ghosts (*pretas*) condemned to suffer from continual hunger pangs because of their past gluttony. The third level is that of the animal world. Then comes rebirth as a human being. This is the most favorable rebirth because its mixture of joy and suffering can lead the soul to the realization of impermanence and the search for a way out of the cycle of *samsara*. The fifth level is that of the *asura*, a race of giants who are forever waging war with each other. The highest level is that of the *devas*,

Jizo. As Buddhism became more popular, there developed the idea of a tribunal to judge the dead and the possibility of mitigating the verdict through the intercession of a divine advocate, the bodhisattva Kshitigarbha (Chinese: Dizang; Japanese: Jizo).

celestial beings who delight in innumerable pleasures, the result of the good karma they have accumulated. But eventually this good karma is exhausted, and they fall down to a lower destiny. In the course of time new, more lenient visions of the afterlife were grafted onto this schema: the Tushita heaven of Maitreya, the buddha of the future, and especially Amitabha's (Japanese: Amida) Pure Land. These paradises, unlike the celestial realms of the *devas*, were conceived of as permanent abodes. Even though the soul's accumulated merit would eventually be exhausted, it did not tumble back down to the lower worlds of suffering. Despite Buddhism's sometimes frightening descriptions of the afterlife, the net effect was to domesticate death, to make the unknown more familiar. For the Chinese, whose lives were given over to administrative routines, the idea of an infernal bureaucracy, despite its Kafkaesque quality, must have been somehow reassuring.

All the same, some uneasiness has persisted concerning the uncertain region that separates the here and now and the hereafter. First of all, there are worries about those spirits who died normal deaths but who, languishing in hell, might seek by some malediction to bring themselves to the attention of the living and encourage them to intercede through devotions and prayers on their behalf.

If most beings who obtain rebirth in one of the six destinies only reap a fate they have created for themselves, the victims of sudden undeserved deaths seem exceptions to this rule. A cruel destiny can cut off a life before its prime, depriving the soul of its legitimate expectations of life and happiness. Such is the case with the deaths of children, women who die in childbirth, virgins, and those born into the lowest levels of the social order. Their fates seem to suggest that the mechanism of transmigration itself can seize up.

Souls in pain, condemned to wander in an in-between state, can come to trouble the peace of the living. Their very existence is a grain of sand in the wheel of karma. In these

Japanese Buddhist cemetery.

Below: *One of the two acolytes of the King of Knowledge, Fudo (Sanskrit: Acala), holding a vajra (thunderbolt scepter) ritual object in tantric Buddhism.*

cases, it is necessary to take extreme precautions with special, lengthy rituals, for example, the funerary rites surrounding the closing of the tomb of a woman who died in childbirth, as well as those performed for an untouchable. Particularly dangerous are returning spirits — fortunately they are quite rare — called in Japanese *onryo* (malefic spirits) or *goryo* (august spirits), who are capable of provoking large-scale catastrophes such as epidemics, droughts or crop failures. The only way to appease these spirits is to found a cult in their honor, to contribute to their divinization.

The hungry ghosts. The phantom doubles of stray dogs and the unfortunate victims of famine, "hungry ghosts" wander unseen among humans never able to satisfy the hunger that gnaws at them. In China, the "little brothers" — the euphemism by which they are known — were the object of such ceremonies such as the "rite of the burning mouth," referring to the fact that all the food they eat immediately bursts into flame. In Japan during the Kamakura period, however, their representation became hallucinatory with the vogue for illustrated scrolls dedicated to the hungry ghosts (*gaki-emaki*).

Wat Phra That Doi Suthep. Chiang Mai, Thailand.

Below: *Pagoda of Ruvanvellisaya, Anuradhapura, Sri Lanka. The word "pagoda" derives from the Sanskrit* garbha-dhatu, *meaning "plan or element of the womb."*

The cult of relics and stupas is unquestionably one of the most important features of Buddhism. Before his death, the Buddha was said to have instructed his disciples to burn his body and distribute his remains among the faithful, who were to place them in stupas. The process of sharing his relics was not an easy one. Several kingdoms fought with each other over the honor of claiming his relics. In any event stupa reliquaries soon became distinguishing marks of the Buddhist landscape. The emperor Ashoka was responsible for a particularly ambitious construction program. The eight principal stupas associated with important events in the life of the Buddha soon became major pilgrimage sites.

Beginning in the seventh century, clay tablets inscribed with a formula in verse on the conditioned nature of all things were housed inside stupas. The formula, itself a kind of verbal relic, took the place of corporeal remains.

The physical relics of the Buddha include the remnants of his body that remained intact (teeth, locks of hair), ashes, and small crystalline fragments (*sharira*) somewhat like pearls, which were said to have been produced during cremation and to be harder than diamonds.

The seven major relics of the Buddha are his four canine teeth, his two collarbones, and a piece of his skull. Veneration of these relics can, among other things, modify karma, procure happiness, attract the protection of good deities, guarantee an easy childbirth, and, in the last instance, assure that one will eventually achieve liberation. The relics also have more widely beneficial effects: they can protect whole nations and ensure good harvests. For the laity, the veneration of relics has almost the same results as veneration of the Buddha himself. In particular, their cult promises rebirth in the Pure Land or Tushita heaven. This belief explains the custom of burying the dead alongside the saints which was first practiced in Indian Buddhism. The foremost Japanese example is the cemetery on Mount Koya, which grew up around the tomb of the Shingon

Mummies

An interesting variant of the cult of relics is the veneration of mummies of Buddhist saints. This has something surprising about it given the disdain with which Buddhism regards the body and its declaration of the impermanence of all things. A Buddhist mummy is not so much a *memento mori*, as formal proof that the person whose body has been embalmed realized nirvana in the course of his lifetime and became "a buddha while in this body" (*sokushin jobutsu*). This is in fact the Japanese expression used to designate mummies. (The Chinese opt for the more prosaic, "body of flesh.")

Similar to relics, mummies are charged with a certain spiritual power, which has often sparked the desire to possess them. This is best illustrated by the master Kukai (774–835). Relics at times became the focus of sectarian disputes. Certain schools stole relics to strengthen their own position or weaken that of their opponents. The most celebrated example is the desecration of the tomb of Honen, the founder of the Pure Land sect, by the followers of the Tendai school in 1227. They attempted to destroy Honen's school by throwing his ashes into the Kamo River.

Among the major relics, the fate of the Buddha's tooth preserved in Sri Lanka has been especially eventful. It was taken from the Ceylonese, first by the Tamils and then by the Portuguese, who claimed to have destroyed it, before finally being returned to its original resting place in the monastery at Kandy. Much has also been written about the "celestial" tooth, given by the god Weituo to the master Vinaya Daoxuan, especially after its transfer to China. The Chinese boast of possessing several of the Buddha's teeth.

According to the Japanese monk Ennin, in the middle of the ninth century, four teeth, one of which was the celestial tooth, could be found in the Chinese capital.

Another famous relic is the Buddha's finger, which is conserved in Fengxiang, China. Like the relic in Sri Lanka, it attracted crowds of pilgrims. Various Chinese emperors have capitalized on this source of legitimacy and spiritual power.

In Korea and Japan, just as in China, much of the early success of the imported religion was associated with relics. In Japan, the cult began during the Heian period. Its popularity intensified in the Kamakura period, with the development of the theory of the "Final Law," and its revival of devotion to the figure of the Buddha Shakyamuni.

The relics of Buddhist saints were revered as well as those of the Buddha. The presence of their relics constitutes the ultimate proof of their awakening to

buddhahood. As the importance of this form of devotion increased so did the number of relics. Cremations of saints could provide hundreds or even thousands of relics, which were shared among the faithful, thus ensuring the success of their schools.

Sanctuary of the Buddha's tooth, Sri Lanka. Although in principle the Buddha disappeared upon entering into final nirvana, his presence is retained in his relics, which have the power to confer liberation. Funerals symbolically reproduce Shakyamuni's awakening, because all funerary rituals produce, after death, a buddha.

case of the master Chan Huineng (d. 713), whose mummy is preserved in the monastery of Nanhua near Canton. Following Chinese tradition, this mummy was threatened on several occasions. In 722, a Korean attempted to steal it. Chinese sources confirm

that the attempt failed, while Korean sources assure us that theft did in fact take place. They claim that Huineng's head now rests in a monastery in Korea.

nonetheless soulless. This iconoclastic tendency was more fully developed in the Chan school of Chinese Buddhism.

In actuality, however, the great bulk of Buddhist practice belies these doctrinal pronouncements. Icons were integral to the spiritual life of Buddhist monasteries; they were intermediaries between the visible and invisible worlds, at the same time seeing and seen, active and passive. The icon served primarily as a receptacle or support for the deity, and provided an object of concentration for the priest and the practitioner.

For the devotee as well as for the priest, icons had transformative power. In India spectators were thought to benefit by simply beholding such a powerful object. By sharing in its essence they were purified and brought to a higher level. The power of Buddhist icons, however, depended not only on their inherent force but on the karma and faith of the

devotee as well. Their benefits become activated only when certain subjective and objective conditions are united.

In China since before the introduction of Buddhism, statues were regarded as living beings, and in the Japanese tradition there are numerous examples of statues sweating, crying, moving, walking, and even flying. Throughout Asia, the animation of statues presupposes the ritual of "opening the eyes." The rite of piercing also brings ancestral tablets or funerary stele to life, even though these non-anthropomorphic objects were never credited with the same mobility as icons.

In the Mahayana ritual of ordination as it developed in China, and more so in Japan, the aspirant had to take a vow, not before invisible rather than visible, teachers, that is, the buddhas and bodhisattvas of the ten directions, made present by their icons — or simply

The earliest forms of Buddhism were aniconic. In the Mahayana tradition as well, many texts affirm that since all things are essentially empty, images of wood or stone do not have the slightest efficacy, and it is therefore useless to make offerings to them. Even if it is meritorious to venerate images since one cannot worship the Buddha in person, the images are

Above: Statue at Wat Yai Chai Mongkhon, Ayutthaya, Thailand.

Below: Small clothed Buddha. Temple in the courtyard of the royal Palace of Phnom Penh, Cambodia.

The first image of the Buddha. According to legend, the first statue of the Buddha was made on the orders of King Udayana when the Buddha departed to the heaven of Indra to preach the Dharma to his mother, Maya. The story tells how the statue came to

greet the Buddha on his return. The statue was more than a simple replica; it was in some sense a double, animated by the Buddha's power.

Similarly, the famous Burmese image of Mahamuni (the Great Sage) at Mandalay was

thought to have been erected during the Buddha's lifetime and animated by his power. It played an important role in assuring the protection of the Burmese royal house by Buddhism.

through visualization. Ordination did not take effect until auspicious signs manifested to the aspirant, who had undergone a long process of confessing his faults. (That period could last from a week up to a year.)

It should be recognized that the major rituals of Mahayana Buddhism (teaching, meditation, ordination, and confession) were closely tied to the presence and visualization of icons of buddhas and bodhisattvas. Their importance has led some to hypothesize that Buddhist iconography has its origin in the role icons played in rites of confession.

The animation of Buddhist icons is a process that can be reduced to five ritual stages:

1. Transmission of the efficacy of a powerful established icon to one or more new icons.

2. Consecration, which corresponds to an esoteric initiation, birth, royal consecration, and entry

into monastic orders.

3. Inspiration, whereby through incantations one or more monks exhort a buddha to descend into the icon, or transfer into the statue some of their own energy accumulated through their practice of ritual and meditation.

4. Depositing relics (*sharira*) or other cult objects in a cavity hollowed out of the body or of the

pedestal on which the icon stands.

5. "Opening the eyes."

This last step is performed by piercing the pupils of the icon with a needle. In some instances the priest avoids the icon's gaze, because its first glance is too powerful. Instead, he uses a mirror in which he sees its reflection.

Longmen, near Luoyang, China.

Below: *Vairocana, the cosmic buddha. Todaiji, Japan.*

Opening of the eyes.
The ritual of "the opening of the eyes" was practiced in India by both Buddhists and Hindus. Descriptions of this practice can be found in esoteric Indian texts that were translated into Chinese during the time of the Tang dynasty and in

Japanese chronicles issued for the consecration of the statue of Vairocana, the cosmic buddha, in Todaiji in 753.

The arhat Ananda, the Buddha's favorite disciple. Dunhuang, China.

Below: *The arhat Kashyapa, the first patriarch of Buddhism. Dunhuang, China.*

After the Buddha's final nirvana, his teachings continued to spread thanks to the zealous efforts of his disciples, who came to be known by the title "arhat" (saint). According to early Buddhist doctrine, this was the highest state that a human being could achieve, as the status of buddha belonged only to Shakyamuni. There is only space to mention a few of the best-known arhats: Kashyapa (called the Great — Mahakashyapa), the Buddha's chosen successor; Ananda, the Buddha's cousin, who recited his sermons from memory and was instrumental in having women accepted in the community; Upali, expert on the details of monastic life; Shariputra, specialist in meditation; and Maudgalyayana, celebrated for his supernatural powers. Maudgalyayana's legend played an important role in the development of funerary rites in China and Japan. The absence of female arhats is to be noted, although Mahaprajapati Gautama, the Buddha's adopted mother and the first nun, has been considered an arhat, and even in certain later texts a female buddha.

In contrast to the ideal of the arhat, which characterizes earlier forms of Buddhism, the Mahayana tradition posits the ideal of the bodhisattva, whose primary quality is compassion. The bodhisattva's compassion inspires him to remain in the world to work for the liberation of all beings, rather than to seek his own salvation in nirvana. Early Mahayana texts adopt a fairly critical attitude toward the arhats. Thus, the *Vimalakirti-sutra*, whose protagonist is a notable laic, Vimalakirti, tends to ridicule the disciples of the buddha for their narrowness of spirit and their misunderstanding of the goals of Buddhist practice.

As a reaction to this largely negative picture of the Hinayana arhat, and no doubt to share the prestige that certain currents of Buddhist thought accorded to the bodhisattvas, there arose in China an entirely new conception — a Mahayana arhat. His image was largely influenced by that of the Taoist Immortal, and he is often pictured accompanied by wild animals.

Mulian (Maudgalyayana) is an altogether unique case. This arhat played a significant role in the development of Buddhism in China, where he was highly esteemed as a shining example of filial piety, and in this regard the equal of any Confucian. Whereas Confucian teachings particularly honored the father, the Buddhists especially revered the mother.

The cult of the arhats (Chinese: *luohan*; Japanese: *rakan*) developed in China along two lines: the cult of the sixteen (or eighteen) arhats on the one hand and the cult of the five hundred arhats on the other. These cults seem to have taken hold in the Chan/Zen school before expanding to a broader segment of society. The awakening interest in the group of sixteen arhats was due to the works of the poet and Chan monk, Guanxiu, to whom they appeared in a dream. To these sixteen, two more were soon added, the arhat of the tiger and the arhat of the dragon.

Although they were of

The first two arhats. Kashyapa and Ananda became the first in a long line of patriarchs, a vitally important role in the growth of Buddhism in China and Japan.

Dogen and the arhats. Held by some to be the "philosopher without peer," Dogen was visited by the 16 arhats who appeared on the branches of a pine tree before the gates of his monastery. This showed that Japan was beyond all doubt superior to China, and that the site of his monastery at Eiheiji was equal in holiness to Mount Tiantai (or Mount Hiei its Japanese counterpart, where Dogen underwent his early training).

Indian origin, the arhats were thought to reside on Mount Tiantai, cradle of the sect of the same name. There was said to be a stone bridge on the mountain that could be crossed only by the perfectly pure of heart.

The cult of the arhats spread to Japan during the Kamakura period, notably through the efforts of the two founders of Zen, Eisai and Dogen. Eisai had himself traversed the stone bridge. As for Dogen, he received visits from the arhats in his home at Eiheiji, the monastery he founded in northeastern Japan. His successor, Keizan Jokin, also had conversations with the arhats in his dreams. One of them appeared to him to let him know that another monastery he had just founded on the peninsula of Noto was called to supplant the one in Eiheiji. As one can see, the arhats were not above entering into sectarian disputes.

Along with the cults of groups of arhats (be they sixteen, eighteen, or five hundred) there also existed a cult devoted to a specific arhat, Pindola (Japanese:

Binzuru), sometimes described as the wandering Jew of Buddhism. Because Pindola succumbed to gluttony and abused his supernatural powers, the buddha condemned him to remain in the world rather than follow him into nirvana. Pindola's popularity arose not so much because he exemplified human weakness, as, because in this world deprived of the presence of the Buddha, he remained the sole surviving witness to the golden age in which the Buddha walked the earth.

If he was invited according to certain prescribed forms, notably by offering him a bath, Pindola might condescend to honor religious ceremonies with his presence. He became, in effect, a witness of the purity of the devotees and the efficacy of ritual. One could be sure of his arrival when his imprint was seen on someone's pillow or when one saw footprints in the monastery bathroom showing that someone had taken a bath. Sometimes Pindola would appear without being invited. In

medieval legends sightings of Pindola multiplied: one could meet with him as if by chance, particularly in times of crisis. His strange appearance would give him away, particularly his long white eyebrows that covered his face.

Tibetan tangka representing an arhat. 18th century, Museum of Oriental Art, Rome. In Mahayana Buddhism, arhats were replaced by bodhisattvas.

Below: *The arhat Binzuru (Pindola), the "wandering Jew" of Buddhism. Nara, Japan.*

Binzuru.
In Japan, Binzuru (Chinese: Pindola) has become a kind of deity of good luck and happiness, sometimes confused with the bodhisattva Jizo, protector of children. His statue, like that of Jizo, is decorated with red baby bibs and

placed in the main entrance of temples. Popular devotion to this deity is such that he is called "the Buddha that one caresses (nade-botoke): that is, the faithful touch the statue and then touch diseased parts of their bodies, to secure his healing

power. The Meiji emperors tried to put a stop to this practice for reasons of hygiene but had to abandon their attempt in the face of popular opposition.

The Bodhisattvas

In early Buddhism, the term "bodhisattva" designated the Buddha Shakyamuni in his incarnations prior to his awakening. Mahayana Buddhism redefined the term. Now bodhisattvas were considered saviors. The bodhisattva's career, the long road that began with an initial thought of awakening (bodhicitta) and led at last to final liberation, was said to endure for three great cosmic cycles (kalpas). Its broad lines are well known: an initial vow to become a buddha, devotion to the buddhas, self-sacrifice, practice of yoga, prediction of future buddhahood, residence in Tushita heaven, miraculous birth in a buddha field, and final awakening. Following this new conception, all aspirants could become bodhisattvas and finally attain buddhahood. In practice the idea that the bodhisattva's compassion causes him to be reborn over and over to seek the liberation of all living beings served as a validation of the role of the laity in Buddhism. Paradoxically, the belief in the presence of bodhisattvas in this world caused Buddhism to become increasingly theistic and devotional. Rather than seeking to become a bodhisattva, by developing the buddha-nature within, the aspirant could hope to attain liberation without too much effort by placing his faith in a powerful and compassionate bodhisattva.

Mahayana offers two fairly distinct conceptions of the bodhisattva. One is an awakened being who delays his entrance into final nirvana to save others. His compassion keeps him in a world governed by passion — in contradistinction to those buddhas who, having entered nirvana, are no longer in theory part of the world and hence cannot participate in its affairs. According to the second, later conception, this distinction becomes blurred. bodhisattvas are regarded as quasi-divine beings endowed with all the powers of a buddha.

Moreover, certain buddhas such as Amitabha (Japanese: Amida) and Bhaishajyaguru (Japanese: Yakushi, the "healing Buddha") by virtue of vows they took when they were simple bodhisattvas, continue to provide help to living beings. From this point of view, it is hard to distinguish them from bodhisattvas.

The most popular of all the bodhisattvas is Avalokiteshvara (Chinese: Guanyin; Japanese: Kannon). Originally male, Avalokiteshvara became, under circumstances that remain obscure, a powerful female deity of compassion and fertility in China. He/she appears in the world in many different forms (animal or human, reassuring or frightening, pure or sensual) to work for the salvation of all beings. Thus, Avalokiteshvara transformed himself into Senayaka, a goddess, to seduce and conquer Vinayaka, the elephant-headed god of obstacles.

As a feminine deity, Guanyin/Kannon epitomizes the ideal of

Guanyin.

In China, Guanyin is sometimes identified as Yang Guifei, the concubine of the Tang emperor Xuanzong. The theme of Guanyin as courtesan is found throughout China. She known as the "wife of Mr. Ma" (Malang fu), who seduces men to lead them to the supreme joy of awakening. According to some traditions, the wife of Mr. Ma dies on her wedding day before consummation of the marriage. In others, once married she proceeds to sleep with all men, delivering them from the bondage of their desires. These legends, which were widespread in monastic communities, seem to have offered the monks a way of sublimating the sexual desires that their asceticism denied them. In some cases, they could be used to justify male homosexuality, as in motherhood. She is revered as the giver of new life and the protector of children. She is petitioned by those seeking to enter into marriage or to reestablish conjugal harmony. The cult of Guanyin/Kannon as a goddess who facilitated conception and eased the pains of childbirth expanded greatly throughout the Middle Ages. There was a famous story of an empress who prayed to the bodhisattva for an easy delivery and was rewarded by a male heir. After the interdiction of Christianity at the beginning of the seventeenth century, many Japanese Christians, forced into apostasy, continued to practice their religion by substituting the image of Kannon holding an infant in her arms for that of Mary.

In some cases, the legends surrounding Avalokiteshvara seemed to justify the narrow roles of wife and mother in which the rigidly patriarchal societies of China and Japan confined women. In this regard, the legend of

Miaoshan no doubt had the greatest impact.

This bodhisattva played an essential role in Japanese and Korean Buddhism. In medieval Japan, women were often barred from public worship. The principal temples dedicated to Avalokiteshvara were places of pilgrimage open to all, without regard to sex or rank. These temples were centers for the practice of healing by means of dreams or visions. Kannon was revered not only for bringing children, but also for bestowing dreams on aspirants during retreats called *komori*. This practice consisted of a retreat in which the faithful shut themselves up in a sacred place for a predetermined period (one night, three nights, a week, or more) to receive prophetic dreams or favorable visions granted by a bodhisattva, buddha, or god. The importance of this phenomenon in medieval Japan ought not be underestimated.

In Tibet, as in China, numerous saints were considered to be avatars of Avalokiteshvara. This is

the case with the Dalai Lama, as well as the Chan patriarch, Bodhidharma. It is equally true of numerous local Japanese divinities, such as the goddess Hakusan, protector of children.

Fukukensaku Kannon, one of the principal forms of the bodhisattva Avalokiteshvara. Hokkedo, Todaiji, Japan. To save all sentient beings, the bodhisattva took 33 principal forms.

the story in which Kannon appears to a Japanese priest in the guise of a handsome adolescent boy and enjoys an idyllic rendez-vous with him as a reward for his meritorious acts.

The legend of Princess Miaoshan.
When Miaoshan refused to marry and decided to enter into a convent, her father, mad with rage, had her killed. During her sojourn in the next world she learned that her father had fallen victim to a horrible

disease because of his crime. Without hesitation, Miaoshan sacrificed herself to save him. Her sacrifice touched the gods, who elevated her to a divine status, making her the bodhisattva Guanyin.

Statue of Bodhidharma. Shaolin Monastery, China. This Indian monk, considered to be the first patriarch of Zen Buddhism, is venerated in Japan under the name of Daruma.

If the metaphysical buddhas, Mahayana doubles of the historical Buddha, remained for the most part abstract, there was another figure, Bodhidharma, whose image in the Buddhism of the Far East also came to serve as a double of the Buddha. Bodhidharma was an Indian monk, the first "Chinese" patriarch of the Chan school, which was originally known as the school of Bodhidharma. He is popularly considered to be an arhat and as an avatar of Avalokiteshvara. The image of the patriarch, his features displaying intense determination, won great success in China and Japan, particularly in the Chan/Zen school, where he is venerated as the Buddha's equal. As has already been mentioned, when Jesuit missionaries first encountered Bodhidharma under his Chinese name, Damo (Dharma), they saw he was a distorted version of Thomas, the Apostle of the Indies. Did Bodhidharma not come "from the West" to preach a mystical doctrine that seemed to them closely akin to Christianity?

According to legend, Bodhidharma was the son of a king of southern India. Having realized the truth of Mahayana, he departed for China in a burst of missionary fervor and arrived in Canton at the beginning of the sixth century. His encounter with Liang Wudi (r. 502–549), a sovereign who prided himself on his many good works, was a short one. When Bodhidharma declared that works were of no value, the king was displeased, and the Indian master decided to withdraw.

This episode became the basis for one of the favorite koans of Chan/Zen. Crossing the Yangtze (on a reed, according to legend), Bodhidharma traveled to northern China, where he took up residence on Mount Song (not far from the eastern capital, Luoyang). There he practiced meditation in a cave facing a wall for nine years without interruption. This prolonged period of contemplation gained him several disciples, among whom was Huike, who was to become the second patriarch. His devotion was such that he cut off his own arm as proof of his zeal.

Believing that he had accomplished his mission,

Daruma dolls.
These dolls are talismans that are thought to ease the pain of childbirth, increase the harvest, and generally ensure the prosperity of those who possess them. As a god of happiness, Daruma presides over many aspects of daily life (domestic safety, business affairs, electoral campaigns) and plays an important role in Japanese art and culture. Sometimes Daruma is portrayed by two dolls known as, "Mr. and Mrs. Daruma."

He is even represented in the company of a courtesan, and since prostitutes know as he does how to take a fall, they have come to be named Daruma.

Another rite linked with Daruma dolls is known as the opening of the eyes. This is done to obtain the deity's protection by a kind

Bodhidharma allowed himself to be poisoned by his rivals. Shortly after his death, a Chinese emissary returning from India said that he had met the master on the Pamir plateau. His tomb was opened and found to be empty. It was therefore concluded that Bodhidharma was a sort of immortal in the Taoist tradition, and that his death had only been a feint. He was also associated with a mysterious figure at Shaolin Monastery, known for its martial arts tradition. Thus he was credited as the founder of Shaolin boxing, the ancestor of kung-fu and other martial arts.

According to later legend, Bodhidharma did not return to India but traveled to Japan. This version was propagated by the Tendai school, which was brought to Japan by Saicho (767–822). The legend associates Bodhidharma with Prince Shotoku Taishi. Prince Shotoku, considered an incarnation of the Tiantai master Nanyue Huisi (515–577), one day met a strange beggar at the foot of

Mount Kataoka (in the prefecture of Nara) and exchanged a poem with him. The identification of the beggar with Bodhidharma rested upon another legend that stated Bodhidharma and Nanyue Huisi met on Mount Tiantai the birthplace of the Tiantai/Tendai school. At that meeting, Bodhidharma predicted that the two of them would meet again in Japan. At the beginning of the Kamakura period, a school named after Bodhidharma (Japanese: Darumashu) grew up within the Tendai school, even before Eisai and Dogen brought Zen to Japan.

But it was primarily in the popular imagination that the figure of Bodhidharma flourished in Japan. In the Edo period, Daruma became a god who protected children and guarded against the pox. He was portrayed in the form of a talismanic doll, made of papier-mâché, crippled and shaky, who, according to an old saying, "fell seven times but got up eight."

Ink on paper representing Bodhidharma (Daruma) in sitting meditation (zazen). *Nojiri Michiko collection, Rome.*

Below: *Daruma dolls covered with inauspicious horoscopes, whose effects they are thought to neutralize. Daruma-dera, Kyoto, Japan.*

of spiritual extortion. According to folklore tradition, the dolls were originally blind, and, as in the case of purely Buddhist icons, the eye-opening ceremony animates them. But there is a difference. They are given only one eyeball. The second one is

not painted on until the petitioner's wish is granted or enterprise completed. This ritual became so widespread that it is now an indispensable part of electoral victories in Japan.

Unfavorable Japanese horoscopes (omikuji) *that are pasted up in Shinto shrines and Buddhist temples to neutralize their ill effects.*

Buddhism may be known in the West for its philosophical insights and meditation techniques, but its arsenal of magical powers was what first won over legions of the faithful. When the cult of the Buddha was introduced in Tibet, China, and Japan, it was first of all that of a god more powerful than the local deities. Correspondingly its representatives, the monks, were sought after for their thaumaturgic powers. Buddhist magic is based upon six supernatural powers (*abhijna*). The traditional list is as follows: the power to overcome obstacles, fly, tame wild animals, and transform oneself at will; the divine eye, which sees the deaths and rebirths of all living beings; the divine ear, which hears all the sounds of the universe; the ability to read the minds and motives of others; the memory of one's own and others' previous lives; and, most important, the awareness of the destruction of all defilements, the end of ignorance, which is the goal of buddhahood. Only the last power is specific to Buddhism. This tendency toward the magical was present in Buddhism from its beginnings, but it was developed by Mahayana teaching and reached its fruition in the Vajrayana tradition. Nonetheless, the attitude of early Buddhism toward the use of magical powers was ambivalent. Even though the buddha accomplished miracles on numerous occasions, he condemned his follower Pindola for displaying his powers in public. Whereas in the Mahayana tradition magical powers were regarded as a by-product of meditation and indicative of a certain level of spiritual attainment, in tantric Buddhism they were openly sought for their own sake.

These powers were sought first of all for the protection of the state. For example, when the Mongols, who were not under themselves

Buddhists, tried to invade Japan in the twelfth century, Buddhist priests were entrusted with the care and protection of the realm. They were to repel the enemy through their prayers and incantations. One of them, Eizon, invoked the "divine winds" and asked them to destroy the Mongol fleet — while sparing all the passengers. Apparently, the gods answered his prayer, but without taking into account Eizon's spirit of compassion. The Mongol fleet was devastated on two separate occasions by storms that could only be seen as providential (at least by the Japanese).

Buddhist powers were invoked for collective as well as individual ends: to protect the emperor and the people, to prevent calamities, to obtain immediate benefits, and to exorcise demons. Certain priests, called protector-monks, were responsible for the person of the emperor and the prosperity of the imperial family. They would

Vajrabodhi.
Legend has it that the tantric master Vajrabodhi practiced a rite of divination for a princess who was at death's door. He chose two seven-year-old girls from the palace and bade them to lie down on the ground. Entering a state of *samadhi*, he ordered the girls to seek out Yama, the king of the underworld, and bring back the vital spirit of the princess.

Soon after, the princess returned to life, and the emperor made Vajrabodhi a knight. But his joy did not last. The princess informed him that she was obliged to return to the other world, for it was there her destiny lay. She died shortly thereafter. Nonetheless, the emperor was so impressed by Vajrabodhi's display of power that he became his disciple.

go so far as to watch that imperial lovemaking was fertile and childbearing was easy. The birthdays of the imperial family were celebrated in all of the monasteries of China and Japan. For the mass of people, exorcisms were particularly important, since it was believed that malevolent deities (goryo) caused the plagues and other calamities that routinely threaten agrarian communities. Through their offerings, the monks had to appease or vanquish these spirits, according to their powers.

Divination played a particularly important role in uncovering the hidden causes of maladies and calamities. It made use of an arsenal of techniques that included astrology and possession, practiced primarily by tantric Buddhists. Following this tradition, rituals were used to invoke demons through a medium, usually a child. This sort of exorcism was effective in curing illness and more particularly in warding off disasters. Various nefarious powers could also be invoked through the use of astrology or by repeating certain mantras. Buddhist astrology in the Far East was a blend of Indian and Chinese traditions. Divination was generally considered only a stage in the process of exorcism. Often, the demon who possessed the body of the ailing person was forced into the body of a medium, from which it could be more easily dispatched. Numerous plays of Noh theater turn on such cases of demonic possession. In some instances dolls were used as surrogates for sick young children, frequent victims of evil spirits. After the spirit was chased into the body of the doll, it was eliminated by offering the doll to a temple. One can still view the wonderful collection of dolls in the Doll Temple (Hokyoji) in Kyoto.

Exorcism was also practiced using talismans and amulets. In certain very serious cases, the recommended method was to seek ordination and then return to one's ordinary life once the danger had passed. For this reason, many mothers-to-be received the tonsure (or often a half-tonsure) before going into labor, since childbirth was a dangerous undertaking. The certificate of ordination, which made the person a child of the Buddha and thus promised final deliverance, became itself a powerful talisman that often could only be had for a very high price. Other Buddhist talismans, relics of earlier Taoist practice, included scraps of paper on which were copied passages from the sutras or particularly efficacious incantations. These were burned, and the ashes were then swallowed. The effectiveness of charms, amulets, and talismans depended not only on the objects themselves, but also on the monks who invested them with power through incantation and meditation.

Box of tickets for divination. Nigatsudo, Nara, Japan. To consult the oracle, the petitioner shakes the box until a numbered ticket falls out. This is then presented to a priest, who casts a horoscope based on it. If the horoscope presages ill fortune, the ticket can be hung on the branches of a sacred tree to annul its effect. At all times and all places in Asia, divination has been one of the essential tools in getting through an existence that is when all is said and done in the hands of the gods.

Below: *The bodhisattva Myoken, symbol of the Pole Star. Museé Guimet, Paris.*

Myoken.
Originally a Taoist divinity, the bodhisattva Myoken became one of the principal figures of Buddhist astrology in the Far East. She was looked upon as the god of the North Star, considered in Chinese astrology to be the ruler of heaven, the fixed point. Her equivalent on earth was the emperor, the Son of Heaven. Around him turned the seven stars of the Great Bear (hokuto). She became a bodhisattva in China and her cult, known in Japan in the seventh century, flourished in the Tendai school during the Heian period. This syncretic cult contained elements of Taoism (the Way of yin and yang; Japanese: Onmyodo), Buddhism, and Shintoism.

Naga. *Khmer statue, Museé Guimet, Paris. According to legend, the protection the Buddha received from the serpent king was a recognition of his spiritual authority by the older earth gods. As water gods, the dragons and nagas played a crucial role in the prosperity of the country. It became the job of Buddhist priests to invoke them to ensure rain.*

Below at right: *Painted wooden dragon from a temple in Chiang Mai, Thailand.*

Buddhism has often been seen as essentially atheistic. However, the arrival of Buddhism did not signal the "twilight of the gods"; on the contrary, one could even argue that each of the cultures in which it took root witnessed a resultant renewal of its local pantheon.

The Great Perfection of Wisdom Treatise, attributed to Nagarjuna, referred to Hindu theism only to criticize it. He stated that Hindu gods, such as Vishnu and Brahma, who were supposed to be creators of the universe, were in fact destroyers of the law of dependent arising of all phenomena. But Buddhist authors could not remain insensible to the appeal of their rivals, and although they began by rejecting the major gods of Hinduism, they ended by enlisting or converting many local deities, whether by choice or by force. This process was facilitated by the similarities in the cosmologies of both religions and by the otherworldly tendencies that grew up in some Buddhist sects. It was further encouraged by the fact that, according to Hindu doctrine, the Buddha was an avatar of Vishnu, even though his mission was to lead the wicked into error and bring the heretics (the Buddhists) to their ruin.

It was within the context of Mahayana teaching that Hinduism exercised its greatest influence. This convergence explains to some degree the disappearance of Buddhism from India or at least its partial reabsorption into Hinduism.

The Hindu pantheon grafted onto Buddhism (or vice versa) was going to experience renewed success in Japan and Tibet. This was especially true with Japanese tantra. In contrast to Buddha Vairocana (Dainichi), who was revered as the principal object of the cult (*honzon*, literally, the "fundamental object of veneration") and was believed to be enthroned at the center of two tantric mandalas (the womb-pattern mandala and the diamond-pattern mandala), certain rituals focused on secondary deities ("particular objects of veneration"). Though of lesser stature, they were formidable nonetheless. Whereas the personality of the buddhas was regarded as basically beneficent (if somewhat distant), those of these more accessible beings were necessarily more ambivalent. By means of appropriate rituals, they could be made to procure immediate gratification for their devotees.

This is why, from the beginning of the tenth century, the number of special, limited sects was seen to multiply. A few particularly significant examples such as those of Fudo, Kangiten, and Daikoku are sufficient to illustrate the point. The King of Knowledge, Fudo

Kangiten. Vinayaka (Japanese: Kangiten) was also called the god of pleasure. Although he was never fully embraced by the orthodoxy, he nevertheless had considerable influence in medieval Japan. He came to represent the cosmic dynamism, the union of the two fundamental principles, in Chinese thought, yin and yang. God of obstacles, which he could worsen or remove as he wished, he is also identified with the *Dosojin*, indigenous deities of crossroads and boundaries, often represented by a male-female couple. He is also sometimes identified with the primordial couple, Izanagi and his sister Izanami, who in Shinto mythology are the progenitors of Japan.

(Sanskrit: Acala, literally the immovable) is without doubt the most representative. Fudo is an angry manifestation of Dainichi, symbolizing the immutability of resolutions. His appearance in wrathful form, is to meant to subdue the forces of evil. He is often represented accompanied by two adolescents (doji), Kongara and Seitaka (Sanskrit: Kimkara and Seitaka). He protects ascetics and helps the faithful fulfill their vows. His martial character made him one of the tutelary deities of the warrior class.

If the great gods of Hinduism had little direct influence on Indian Buddhism, indirectly the image of Shiva in sexual union with his partner (symbolizing the divine creative energy) had a considerable influence on tantric imagery and art. This is how the son of Shiva, the elephant god Ganesh, came to have a second career in the Shingon school of Japanese Buddhism, in the form of a two-headed god combining good and evil. He was represented by two human figures with elephant heads making "the beast with two backs." The sexual symbolism of this representation brings us back to the legend of Vinayaka, according to which he was converted — in fact seduced and domesticated — by the bodhisattva Avalokiteshvara. Taking the form of Vinayaka's sister, Senayaka, the bodhisattva, in exchange for sexual favors, elicited his promise that he would no longer harm living beings.

The cult of "particular objects of veneration," with its roots in tantra, became one of the dominant traits of Buddhist practice in medieval Japan. This form of Buddhism was characterized by its belief in thaumaturgic powers and the efficacy of magical rituals. It was also noted for its close association with the ruling powers. In a system in which the continuance of the imperial line relied upon complex matrimonial strategies, the role played by these cults was a far cry from Buddhism's spiritual and salvational ideals. Monks

were chosen not for their virtue but for their ability to further the aims of the imperial family by assuring the birth of male heirs. They were even called upon to destroy the emperor's enemies through their rituals.

Fudo Myoo (Acala Vidyaraja), one of the five great kings of the science of magic. Museé Guimet, Paris. Fudo's body is either blue or black, surrounded by an aureole of flames. He has two prominent canine teeth, one curving up and the other down. He holds a sword in his right hand and a rope in his left.

Daikoku. The Hindu god Shiva appears in Japanese Buddhism in the form of Daikoku, the Great Black One (translation of a Sanskrit epithet for Shiva). The earliest representations portray him in his most terrible aspect. Because of a transcription error on the part of Kukai, the founder of the Shingon school, Daikoku was written as the "Great Country", identifying him with Okuninushi (literally, "Lord of the Great Country"), god of civilization, abundance and fertility. Thus, through phonetic and mythological confusions, Daikoku came to figure in the pantheon of benevolent deities. Notably, he was placed among the group of the seven gods of happiness (shichi fukujin) in the Edo period and acquired the characteristic traits of these divinities.

Ceremony in a Tendai monastery. Repentance is the indispensable preliminary for all ritual.

Below: *Monk sweeping the courtyard in Enryakuji, the grand monastery of the Tendai sect, on Mount Hiei, Japan.*

Rituals and liturgy regulate Buddhist monastic life. One can identify exoteric rites, which are performed for the sake of some external aim, and esoteric rites, which have as their goal the identification of the aspirant with the divinity. Some rites are undertaken on one's own account, others for the sake of another. Buddhist ritual is not limited to the performance of annual, monthly, or daily celebrations during the liturgical year, it is also composed of meditation and various other activities (such as gardening in Zen monasteries) that at first glance appear unrelated to ritual. One can distinguish four types of ritual. In the course of their spiritual practice monks and other aspirants engage in rituals such as summer retreats, the copying of sutras, rites of ordination and confession, intensive periods of meditation (*sesshin*), and manual labor (in Zen monasteries). Then there are ceremonial actions dedicated to the Buddha, the patriarchs, or the founder of a particular monastery, or those held on anniversaries of the Buddha's birth (April 8), his awakening (December 8), and his entry into final nirvana (February 15). Then come rituals specifically designed to ward off calamities; appease malevolent spirits; obtain good fortune, health and material success; secure bountiful harvests and plentiful rains; and guarantee the continuing prosperity of the state. Finally, there are those rituals devoted to transferring merit for the dead and the living. These categories are, however, flexible, and one ritual can serve several purposes.

The basic structure of all ritual follows a sequence of three actions: invoking the deity, making offerings, and returning to the world. All rituals begin by delimiting a sacred space in which divinity can manifest. In exoteric sects such as the Pure Land school, the buddha Amida is perceived as an external reality, a savior; in esoteric Buddhism, such as Zen, the Buddha turns out to be none other than oneself, or let us say one's best self, the buddha-nature within each sentient being. To ask the Buddha to manifest does not have the same meaning or imply the same attitude on the part of the aspirant who asks the buddha Amida to descend from the Pure Land, and the aspirant who seeks his own buddha-nature in meditation. In the latter case one seeks mastery over one's own latent powers, to identify with an immanent Buddha, whose essence is identical to one's own. In the former case one seeks to please a transcendent being who is altogether different and separate from oneself.

The ordination of monks is surely the most important ritual in Buddhism, since it guarantees the perpetuation of the Sangha without

The ritual of the sermon.

During his sermon, the Zen priest poses as an incarnation of the Buddha, thus reenacting the preaching of the Buddha on Vulture Peak Mountain. The ritual of the sermon recapitulates all the other rituals, in that it clearly shows that meditation and the koan create an space of awakening into which a transcendent force descends. All the rites of confession or visualization involve bringing down the buddhas, bodhisattvas, or other Buddhist divinities.

The recitation of the names of the buddhas is thus as much a convocation as an invocation.

which ritual practice would not exist. In the presence of ten officiants, the candidate is asked to respond to a series of varied questions concerning his acceptability. He then declares himself ready to observe the fundamental prohibitions of monastic life and refrain from sexual relations, theft, murder, dishonesty, and boastfulness concerning his mastery of spiritual powers. In the case of a prospective nun, the process is repeated in the presence of the chapter of nuns, and certain additional rules apply. A formal collective confession is preceded by individual confession. With each section of the monastic formula, the enumeration of prohibitions is followed by a threefold question wherein the officiant asks the candidate whether he is free from the mentioned faults. The candidate's silence is taken to signify an affirmative answer. These faults, numbering 250 for monks and 348 for nuns, are enumerated in a formula called *Pratimoksha*. The ritual convocation takes places twice a month, at the full and new moons.

Penitence is essential for the candidate, because without it the necessary purity required cannot be obtained.

In Mahayana Buddhism, a new rite of ordination developed based upon the vows of the bodhisattvas. Following this teaching, ordination no longer requires the presence of ten officiants; the aspirant can become ordained by taking a personal vow. But the process is watched over by invisible buddhas and bodhisattvas who appear to the postulant during contemplation or in a dream. The same acts of contrition are in order. They are offered to the buddhas of the ten directions, represented concretely by a Buddhist icon. This form of ordination was not necessarily easier than the older one. It was not held to be completed until a vision was granted to the candidate, and until that time he had to continue his process of repentance.

As has been indicated, confession for Buddhists is not so much an individual act motivated by remorse and aimed at the absolution

of sins, as a collective act whose goal is the accumulation of merit. It is part of a ritual that includes visualization, fasting, invocation of the buddhas, and prostrations — all undertaken to obtain an auspicious vision or dream. It is not surprising, then, that the ritual takes place in front of an icon (sometimes a stupa), which places the aspirant in the presence of an invisible buddha. In many ways, Buddhism (and not only its esoteric or tantric forms) remains an initiatory religion.

Thai monk performing a ritual. All rituals begin by delimiting a sacred area into which the divinity can descend.

Ordination and contrition. Sometimes one ritual can conceal another. Thus, ordination and confession became purely liturgical ceremonies from which one could expect all sorts of immediate benefits through purification and the elimination of karmic

obstacles. In the case of serious illness the contrition and sometimes the ordination of the sick person was considered the best remedy, or at least the best medicine.

The naga goddess Shanmiao. Nagas (dragons) occupy an important place in Buddhist imagery.

At right: Hariti. Bas-relief Borobudur, Indonesia. There are many deities in the Buddhist pantheon.

Buddhism has often been accused of misogyny, and not without reason. Yet it has always been a refuge for women seeking to escape their unenviable destinies as mothers and wives. In the patriarchal societies of Asia women have often been viewed as a necessary evil, commodities whose only value was to assure the continuation of a family line. Buddhism inherited this ambivalence. The tone was set at the inception of the community of female practitioners. We learn that the Buddha originally refused to accept his adoptive mother, Mahaprajapati, into the monastic order. It was only at the urging of his beloved disciple and cousin, Ananda, that he finally consented to allow this woman, who had raised him as her own son, to become his disciple. At the same time, he imposed draconian conditions on women who chose to enter the Sangha. Nuns had to observe not only the normal rules of monastic life but a series of eight stricter rules that required that nuns, regardless of their age or rank, had to obey monks in all things. Further, the Buddha predicted that with the entrance of women into religious orders, his doctrine would enter a period of decline and vanish altogether within one thousand or fifteen hundred years.

Thus, the orders of nuns were doubly subordinate: to the orders of monks as well as to the rules of the community. Nonetheless, the first nuns seemed to have enjoyed a certain

Hariti. As the protector of children, Guanyin had a longtime rival in the goddess Hariti, a role for which she was an unlikely candidate. According to legend, Hariti was originally an ogress. To convert her, the Buddha hid her child away. The anguish she experienced at the loss of her child made her suddenly realize the horror of her crimes. She resolved from then on to protect children and their mothers.

prestige. That they were considered more or less the spiritual equals of monks is evidenced by the legend of Mahaprajapati and certain poems written by nuns contained in the *Therigatha*.

In time, their situation degenerated. The fact that they were legally and economically dependent upon the orders of monks led to their decline and then disappearance from Theravadan Buddhism. In the countries of the Far East where Buddhism took hold, it was extremely difficult to ordain women, since the rite required the presence of ten already ordained monks and nuns. Nonetheless, orders of nuns proceeded to grow, though not without vicissitudes. They flourish today in Korea and Taiwan, in contrast to Japan, where the orders of nuns have had to confront to their disadvantage the practice of monastic marriage. Though Japanese Buddhism permits monks to marry, nuns are required to remain celibate.

Despite these social inequalities— justified and

even aggravated on a doctrinal level — Buddhism has always exerted a strong attraction for women. It is true that Buddhist teaching condemns women, who were regarded as impure and perverse beings. It even goes so far as to deny the possibility of their attaining enlightenment in their present form. At the same time, however, it offers women the hope of salvation in another world, the Pure Land of Amida. It provides them comfort in the roles they have to play in society by offering them

models such as the bodhisattva Guanyin, archetypal image of feminine compassion.

And for those who could not accept the role that society prescribed for them Buddhism offered a way out. Ultimately convent life constituted a less painful form of servitude than marriage. Today the rise of feminism is calling into question the traditional subjugation of women that has endured at the heart of Buddhism.

A nun in a convent in Nepal.

Below: *Sculpture representing Tara. Indian Museum, Calcutta. Another popular bodhisattva of Indo-Tibetan Buddhism is Tara, who is often linked with Avalokiteshvara. The ambivalent nature of this goddess is characteristic of tantric Buddhism. Sometimes she is seen as a benevolent spirit; at other times she is represented in a terrible guise, destroying her enemies.*

Symbolism of the womb.

One of the rituals that the ascetics of Shugendo, the *yamabushi*, performed on their sacred mountains says a great deal about certain masculine fantasies. It entails a return to the womb, a ritual regression

that consists of penetrating ever more deeply into a cave, the symbol of the divine and maternal womb. In fact, this ritual is only the culmination of the climb, which is completely lived out on the symbolic plane as a kind of gestation. To "enter into the

mountain," the devotee clothes himself in a highly symbolic outfit (one piece signifying the umbilical cord, another the placenta) that makes him into a perfect little embryo.

Buddhism and Utopia

The Buddha sculpted from a rock. Leshan, Sichuan, China.

Below: *Gates of Shinto shrine leading to the mausoleum of Kukai on Mount Koya, Japan.*

Below right: *Sanctuary on Mount Koya, center of the Shingon sect founded by Kukai. Japan.*

As has been noted, the Buddha Shakyamuni is only the latest in a long series of buddhas. Buddhist texts also speak of future buddhas, the best known of whom is Maitreya (Chinese: Mile; Japanese: Miroku). Maitreya is generally considered to be a bodhisattva who is now waiting in the Tushita heaven, as all other buddhas have before him, to return to earth in his final incarnation, before attaining nirvana. His future birth is not determined exclusively by his individual karma; it is also dependent on the cosmic cycle — part of the Hindu legacy to Buddhism. Before Maitreya arrives, Shakyamuni's prophecies regarding the decline of Buddhism and the world have to take effect. Because our world is that of the Final Law, things are going to go from bad to worse. It is only when the worst has passed that the world can look toward a new golden age, in the course of which Maitreya will appear in order to restore the Dharma to its original perfection. Once again, all beings will find it easy to attain enlightenment. That is why the fondest desire of monks in the Middle Ages was to be reborn at the time of Maitreya's return. Some of them resolved to follow in the footsteps of Kashyapa, who at the death of the Buddha Shakyamuni entered into a state of profound meditation, suspending his metabolism to achieve a kind of semi-immortality. The story of Kashyapa's meeting with Maitreya — or at least the version that Shakyamuni, in his omniscience, told his disciples — is worth taking the time to relate.

As already mentioned, the meeting takes place at the end of the present cosmic cycle at which time the world and its inhabitants have rediscovered their original perfection. Humanity has become the race of giants it was at the beginning. It is in this context that Maitreya arrives and begins to preach. One day, he declares to his disciples that the moment has come for him to receive the robe of Shakyamuni from Kashyapa. His disciples accompany him up the mountain where the arhat has waited for countless millennia. When Kashyapa appears to Maitreya and his disciples, they encounter a minuscule figure. Shakyamuni's precious robe hardly covers Maitreya's little finger. Maitreya rebukes his incredulous disciples, teaching them that the size of a man, conditioned by the epoch into which he is born, has nothing to do with his level of spiritual attainment, which is unconditioned. To prove the point, Kashyapa displays supernatural powers that go far beyond anything Maitreya's disciples have achieved.

For those who could not wait for the advent of Maitreya, two other solutions presented themselves: either ascend to Tushita heaven through spiritual exercises and there receive his teachings, or encounter a provisional incarnation of Maitreya in this world. The idea that Maitreya manifests in this world to get started on his work of salvation before the hour of his final rebirth was widely accepted in the Far

Kukai.

According to tradition, the founder of the Shingon sect of Buddhism entered into *samadhi* in 835 C.E. on Mount Koya. He is thought to be there still, immersed in concentration in a sanctuary deep within the mountain.

East. Over the course of centuries various personages were considered to be incarnations of Maitreya. The most famous was a Chan monk of the tenth century known by the nickname of Budai. (Japanese: Hotei, literally, "canvas bag" because he always carried one.) Budai, in popular religious, belief became the "laughing buddha." This great-bellied figure, whom the earliest Western collectors of Chinese art called Pussah (from the Chinese *pusa,* for bodhisattva), is often represented in the company of children. He is worshipped in Japan as one of the seven gods of happiness. In the Edo period in Japan, Maitreya's cult was based, with some local differences, on the "renewal of the world" (*yonaoshi*). According to popular belief, Maitreya will come from across the seas in a boat — recalling the cargo cults of Oceania — to inaugurate an era of prosperity. This is somewhat different from the beliefs of the Shingon school, centered on Mount Koya and the surrounding

sacred mountains of Shugendo. In the pre-modern era, ascetics emulating Kashyapa and Kukai had themselves buried alive to achieve self-mummification. The most celebrated example is that of Miroku Jigikyo, a supposed avatar of Maitreya, who entered into *samadhi* in 1773 at the top of Mount Fuji to mark the arrival of the world of Maitreya. His disciples founded a school called Fujido (the Supreme Way, which puns on the word *fuji*, "without equal", and Mount Fuji). Its goal was the creation of a utopia in this world based on the ideal of androgyny, an ideal marked by its reversal of the traditional sexual hierarchy, notably through transvestism. Despite governmental repression, these ideas were quite popular in the agrarian communities of the Edo period. Other new religions, also of a messianic character, followed and combined with peasant revolts to contribute to the decline of the reign of the Tokugawa and the Meiji restoration.

Maitreya was reported to have reincarnated once again in 1928 in the person of Deguchi Onisaburo, a founder of Omotokyo, one of the principal new religions of present-day Japan. Some of these new religions derive from Buddhism, but most are syntheses of Shinto, Taoist, Confucian, and Christian elements.

The future buddha, Maitreya. Datong Grotto, China.

Below: *Budai, the laughing buddha. Hangzhou, China.*

The vision of Maitreya.
Numerous practitioners over the centuries have reported visiting the palace of Maitreya during initiatory trance states. In a recent case the master Chan Xuyun, after having been mistreated by the

Communist Chinese authorities, fell into a trance in which, he told his disciples, he received wondrous visions of Maitreya.

The bodhisattva Dizang (Jizo), element for a triptych. Sui dynasty, Dunhuang, China. In Central Asia, this bodhisattva was simply one of two acolytes of the Buddha, but in China and Japan he achieved an iconographic and cultic autonomy, becoming one of the most popular figures of the Buddhist hierarchy. Here he makes a gesture of protection.

The Sangha can be defined as a community that shares a common vocabulary of gestures as much as a common doctrine and discipline. In fact, monastic discipline is essentially a matter of holding the correct posture. Monks seek to reproduce the four "majestic attitudes" of the Buddha: walking, standing, sitting, and lying down. Of these the seated posture is the most important: the practitioner must always be in his seat — that is, centered within himself — even when beset by desire.

Sitting meditation (*dhyana*, the Sanskrit term which is rendered into Chinese as "Chan" and into Japanese as "Zen") is not only a principal feature of Chan/Zen; it is the common denominator of all Buddhist practice. It is usually performed in the lotus position; back straight, feet crossed and resting on the opposite thigh, and one hand on top of the other with palms upward, to form the *mudra* of concentration (Sanskrit: *dhyanamudra*).

If *mudras* imply the elevation of the practitioner, prostrations, although they seem to begin with a *mudra*, signify abasement before the buddhas. Whereas the seated position requires a straight posture, in a physical as well as a moral sense, it is preceded by a ritual prostration. At first glance prostration is quite different from the ritual identification with the Buddha that is inherent in meditation or in *mudras*, but it is, in fact, their complement. Performing prostrations requires a certain physical endurance, notably in the series of prostrations that marks the collective ritual of contrition. But the Buddhist rite offers a significant variant to the traditional Chinese salutation of touching the ground with one's forehead.

In this position, the Buddhist raises his hands with palms facing the sky to symbolically invite the Buddha to take him for his pedestal. Although this attitude implies a distinction between the invisible Buddha seated on his human platform and the aspirant, the contact with the divine constitutes a sanctification.

The Buddhist salutation in its various forms (a simple bow with joined hands, or a full prostration) is one of the essential gestures, a "value rendered physical" that, according to Pierre Bourdieu, is capable of "inculcating a cosmological, ethical, metaphysical and political system through such simple injunctions as 'stand up' (or 'bend down')." It serves to define the Buddhist hierarchy.

Another way of expressing respect is through circumambulation (Sanskrit: *pradakshina*). The earliest Buddhist texts

Mudras.
Literally translated as "seals," *mudras* are symbolic gestures. The most simple and basic *mudra* is formed by joining both hands as in Christian prayer (Japanese: *gassho*). This not only symbolizes but realizes the unity of the masculine and feminine principles. The practitioner identifies his body with that of the Buddha and is sanctified by these spiritually significant gestures.

The pilgrim's journey finds an analog in the hands of a clock (or in the annual voyage of the sky around the sun). Thus, the Chinese pilgrim Xuanzang made a tour of India in the seventh century. This circular journey was seen as a symbolic conquest of the four directions, which imply the fifth direction, the zenith. The movement is therefore also an ascension, since it leads to supreme awakening.

Circumambulation of a stupa. Swayambhunath, Kathmandu, Nepal. The disciples of the Buddha turned around him three times, baring their right shoulders. The ritual circumambulation reproduces this early act.

The Buddha seated in mediation under the protection of the naga Mucilinda. Ayudhya Ayutthaya, Thailand.

describe the Buddha's disciples turning around him three times with their right shoulders bared. Ritual circumambulation is nothing more than an imitation of this respectful gesture. But a cosmological significance was quickly grafted onto the ritual involving the four cardinal points, a symbolism magisterially analyzed by Paul Mus in his study of Borobudur.

Circumambulation as a ritual became so important that it began to determine the circuit of pilgrimage from one site to another.

Hierarchy of the Sangha. The Sangha is composed of four groups: monks, nuns, male laics, and female laics. Many texts declare that monks do not have to prostrate to laics or nuns. This issue became problematic in China, where the clerical orders found themselves subordinated to the Son of Heaven, who held supreme authority in both the temporal and spiritual realms. Insofar as he was a member of the laity, the monks thought that they should not be required to prostrate to him. The controversy, which took place in the fourth century, was resolved to the advantage of the emperor. The monks had to bow not only to the emperor, but to his relations as well.

135

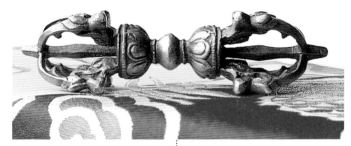

Ritual objects: incense burner, bell, five-pointed vajra.

At right: *Tibetan monks blowing on trumpets. These trumpets, common in Tibetan Buddhist practice, are thought to chase away evil spirits that might interfere with the smooth order of ritual practice.*

Buddhist monks were allowed to possess a certain number of objects considered indispensable for daily life. Soon each of these became charged with a complex symbolic meaning. Along with those used by individuals, a number of objects figure in the life of the community or in communal rituals. In any case, the distinction between the two is never hard and fast, and one object can fill several roles. There are objects specific to a certain school such as the tantric *vajra* (thunderbolt scepter) or the whisk brooms of Zen masters. These latter (Chinese: *fuzi*; Japanese: *hossu*) are made of the hair of boars, yaks, or cows and signify the spiritual authority the master has over his students. They also provide demonstrations of compassion since the teacher uses them to brush insects away without hurting them. Chan writings often refer to the master lifting his whisk broom to let the student know he is ready to begin a discussion.

The rosary (Sanskrit:

Some important ritual objects.
The *kasaya* (Japanese: *kesa*), or monk's frock, is, with the begging bowl, one of six (or eighteen) personal objects permitted to Buddhist monks. Originally, it was a red or brown stole made of stitched-together bands whose number varied according to the function of the kasaya, or the rank of the wearer. In time, the robe of the Dharma evolved into a liturgical vestment worn over one's ordinary clothing, signifying clerical ordination. It was with the coronation of the sixth patriarch, Huineng, that the robe acquired its privileged status in Chan Buddhism.

The begging bowl (*patra*), a symbol of the Dharma, played a vital role in the lives of mendicant monks. In numerous texts, *mala*; Japanese: *nenju*) is comparable to the Christian rosary. It may consist of 18 beads (symbolizing the 18 arhats and sometimes depicting their faces) or, in Japanese tantric practice, 108 (for the 108 afflictions). In the Pure Land sect, a special ritual is practiced in which a group of devotees tell an enormous rosary while reciting the *nenbutsu*.

An object particular to tantric Buddhism is the *vajra* (Tibetan: *dorje*) with one or several points. The *vajra* with one point (or actually two, one on each side of a short handle), is a phallic symbol often coupled with the feminine lotus. Among other forms, the most common are those with three or five points. The latter, in which the points are arranged in the form of a crown or in four points around a central axis, refers to various tantric quinaries, such as the five tantric elements, the five buddhas, or the five wisdoms. At the same time, it represents the human

body with its head, two arms, and two legs. In certain rituals crossed *vajras* represent sexual union.

The role of some objects, such as small sticks, was purely collective. In Indian Buddhism the they served all kinds of quantitative and qualitative functions: to count the participants in the course of communal practices as well as to resolve disputes. In some instances these sticks played a mnemonic role. When decisions had to be made, they were used to count votes or choose between opposing sides. They were also used as lots, when the property of a dead monk had to be divided. Counting sticks played an important role in the major schisms, when the method of determining the majority often aroused suspicions. In the Mahayana tradition, which had been the beneficiary of this proce-dure (and therefore knew the dangers inherent in majority rule) their use to resolve disputes seems to have fallen into disfavor to

the extent that com-munities became more ritualized and authoritarian. In Chan/Zen, for example, they were used almost exclusively for ritual purposes. A more practical use was to count the number of circles made around the sanctuary in the circumambulation rituals that characterized more popular forms of Buddhism. The participant places a stick in a box in front of the altar, each time that ten rounds are completed.

It has been said that tools serve to carry gestures further. Thus, the introduction of the chair into China around the time of the Tang dynasty seems to have been preceded and prepared for by numerous representations, dating from the fifth century, of buddhas seated in Western style, that is, with feet on the ground rather than folded under the body in the customary kneeling position. This posture, which characterized royalty in India, seems in China to have been perceived as an

it stands for the monk himself, to the extent that he risked death if his bowl was accidentally destroyed. There are also numerous references to the Buddha's flying bowl , whose appearance is considered to be a precursor of the expansion of Buddhism.

The pilgrim's staff, a kind of noisemaker fitted with several metal rings (*khakkhara*), is also an important object. The silent pilgrim rattles it to announce his approach. The staff is thought to chase away wild animals and other dangers along the

way. Thence its role in exorcisms. It is the principal attribute of Jizo, who uses it in certain rituals to break down the gates of hell and rescue those dwelling there.

Monk with rosary. This consists of 18 beads (symbolizing the arhats) or in Japanese tantra 108 beads (the number of afflictions).

Below: *Begging bowl. In many texts the bowl is a virtual double of the monk who carries it, and for whom it plays such a vital role.*

effective protection against demons. Representations of the buddha Maitreya, in particular, often show him seated in a chair.

In India, chairs were important furnishings in monasteries. They were originally reserved for eminent monks as a sign of their dignity, in emulation of the monarch's throne. They were also used for meditation. The monk and pilgrim Yijing, in describing Indian customs he observed in his travels in the seventh century India, complained about what he considered a deviation from traditional practice: instead of taking their meals sitting normally on their chairs, the monks he encountered sat cross-legged in the lotus position.

But the lotus position would become the rule for Chinese and Japanese Buddhism. The use of a high seat is often found in Chan/Zen. It is common to see representations of the master giving a sermon seated on a chair with his legs crossed in the lotus position, clothed in a ceremonial robe. Usually, he holds his whisk broom as a symbol of his authority. Likewise, the founder of the Shingon sect, Kukai (Kobo Daishi), is generally depicted in the lotus position on a high chair during a ritual, holding a *vajra* in one hand and a rosary in the other. But in contrast to China, where chairs soon became an integral part of household furnishings, even the influence of Buddhism was not strong enough to impose the use of the chair in Japan. Architecture continued to be organized around the traditional manner of sitting. It was not until the nineteenth century that one began to find chairs in ordinary Japanese homes.

Seated Buddha, carved into rock. Bingling caves, Gansu, China. There exist 183 caves carved into the rocky walls of this narrow valley.

Opposite page: *Interior of Swayambhunath, Kathmandu, Nepal.*

Buddhism and the body. What importance does the physical ideal of the Buddha hold for the ordinary practitioner? There are many different ideas. The most common one, derived from the Mahayana tradition, is that the body is illusory; not only the empirical, physical self, but also the psychosomatic aggregates of which it is composed. To emphasize its ephemeral nature, the body is compared to a drop of water, a mirage, or a shadow. Even when one grants it a minimal existence, it is the subject of all sorts of negative judgments. It is the body that involves us in the incessant turbulence of the karmic retribution. The ascetic's practice is thought to transform his body into that of the Buddha.

Glossary

Amitabha (Japanese: Amida): the buddha of the Pure Land, the main Buddhist paradise.

Ananda: cousin and favorite disciple of the Buddha. After the Buddha entered into final nirvana, Ananda transmitted his message, reciting his teachings from memory.

Arhat: adept who has reached the ultimate stage in the practice of Buddhism; in particular, the close disciples of the Buddha.

Ashoka: Buddhist emperor who reigned over India in the third century BC. His devotion to Buddhism led to the widespread propagation of the religion.

Atman: the Self. In Hinduism the divine spark within everyone that is identified with the Absolute, *Brahman*; in Buddhism, the term is used to designate the illusory self.

Avalokiteshvara (Chinese: Guanyin; Japanese: Kannon): bodhisattva of compassion.

Bodhi (Enlightenment): derives from the root *buddh*, meaning "to awaken." This term in Buddhism denotes the perfect realization of the truth, which causes the cycle of transmigration to end and brings about nirvana.

Bodhisattva: literally "awakened" *(bodhi)* "being" *(sattva)*. The term designates one who out of compassion vows to save all sentient beings before entering nirvana himself.

Brahman: the Absolute in the Vedic religion, which is identical to the *atman*, in each individual.

Buddha: "Awakened One": epithet of Shakyamuni.

Deva: divine beings of the Hindu pantheon. In Buddhism the term refers to those beings who are reborn in paradise, thanks to the good karma they have accumulated, but are still not free of the Wheel of Karma.

Dharma: in Hinduism dharma designates the cosmic, social and religious order. In Buddhism when capitalized, it signifies Buddhist law, both the cosmic order and the Buddha's teaching; when in lower case, it denotes the constituent elements of conventional reality.

Guru: spiritual teacher.

Hinayana (Lesser Vehicle): a somewhat pejorative term used by Mahayana Buddhism to designate its rival school, that of traditional Buddhism (see Theravada).

Kami: gods of the Japanese pantheon. The "way of the *kamis*" designates the relatively recent belief system (definitely not indigenous as is often maintained) of Shintoism.

Karma: recompense for one's actions, entailing a series of transmigrations and rebirths *(samsara)* from which both Hindus and Buddhists try to free themselves through their religious practice.

Koan (Chinese: gong'an): "case" or enigma posed by Chan/Zen masters, that aims to short-circuit the intellect and draw on the powers of intuition.

Kshitigarbha (Chinese: Dizang; Japanese: Jizo): a very popular boddhisattva in Sino-Japanese Buddhism. Guardian of crossroads, he guides the souls of the dead to more favorable rebirths. In Japan he is also honored as the protector of infants and children.

Lama: Tibetan translation of the Sanskrit *guru*.

Maitreya (Chinese: Mile: Japanese: Miroku): the buddha of the future. A messianic cult has grown up around him.

Mahayana (Great Vehicle): a school of thought that developed in India around the beginning of the common era as a reaction against the conservatism of the Hinayana schools.

Mara: the Buddhist tempter, also the god of death.

Naga: a supernatural being in the form of a snake or dragon who has power over water, and, hence, rain.

Nenbutsu (Chinese: nianfo): remembrance of the Buddha, either verbally or mentally, by which the adherents of the Pure Land School invoke the saving grace of Amitabha.

Nirvana: extinction, the destruction of desire and suffering. Nirvana ends the cycle of transmigration (samsara).

Pratitya-samutpada: "conditioned origination." The Buddhist theory of causality. It consists of twelve elements describing the chain of karma, which leads from ignorance to death to rebirth. By retracing one's steps along this path, one can erase the chain of causation and attain nirvana.

Samadhi: this Sanskrit term designates the spiritual state attained in meditation.

Sangha (or Samgha): community of believers instituted by the Buddha consisting of four groups: monks, nuns, laymen and lay women.

Samsara: Sanskrit term for transmigration, the cycle of rebirths conditioned by karma. Nirvana is the deliverance from *samsara*.

Shakyamuni: literally "ascetic of the Shakya," one of the epithets of the Buddha, referring to his clan name.

Sarira (Sanskrit for "body"): physical remains, relics, and more precisely crystalline fragments, that were produced in the cremation of Buddhist saints.

Shingon: esoteric sect of Japanese Buddhism founded by Kukai (774–835). It taught the practice of incantation of mantras.

Shinto: literally, "way of the *kamis*," the gods of the Japanese pantheon.

Shugendo: literally "way of power." Syncretic Japanese school that borrowed from Buddhism and Shintoism. Its adepts sought to attain psychic powers through ascetic practices in the mountains.

Sila: Buddhist moral code, one of the "three disciplines" (along with *samadhi* and *prajna*). In practice it consisted of the 250 rules of the monastic code *(Vinaya)*.

Shunyata: Emptiness, according to Mahayana Buddhism a description of the ultimate nature of reality.

Tantra: religious current in both Hinduism and Buddhism, founded on the study of the certain Sanskrit texts, called *tantras*.

Taoism: Chinese religion said to have been founded by Laozi, based upon the Tao, the principle underlying all phenomena.

Tara: tantric goddess of compassion.

Tathagatha: epithet of the Buddha, who realized the ultimate reality.

Theravada ("way of the elders"): a current within Hinayana Buddhism characterized by its decision to return to the original teachings of the Buddha.

Tripitaka: the "three baskets" of Hinayana Buddhist doctrine: sutras, *Vinaya*, and *Abhidharma* (or *sastras*, scholarly treatises).

Upaya: "skillful means." Because the Buddha and bodhisattvas practiced *upaya*, they could guide aspirants toward deliverance.

Uposatha (Sanskrit: *poshadha*): ceremony centering on the recitation of the monastic code and public confession. It takes place twice a month at the full and new moon.

Vairocana (Japanese: Dainichi): the cosmic buddha of the Vajrayana tradition.

Vajrayana: vehicle of the Vajra (thunderbolt or diamond scepter), the Sanskrit term for tantric Buddhism.

Vedism: archaic religion of India based on the *Vedas*.

Vinaya: Buddhist monastic code.

Zen: Japanese form of Chan Buddhism. Introduced into Japan in the ninth century, it was not formally recognized as a school until some centuries later.

Buddhism today

One ought to take with a grain of salt the numbers advanced by the various Buddhist organizations. They are sometimes exaggerated, sometimes deliberately lowered (as is the case with the figures published by the Chinese government). The population figures here are based on those published in the *International Buddhist Directory* (1985).

1. Theravada tradition:

Approximately 105 million believers
SRI LANKA: 11 million
BURMA: 30 million
THAILAND: 47 million
CAMBODIA: 6 million
LAOS: 3.5 million
To which one must add minorities in China, Bangladesh, India, and Indonesia.

2. Mahayana & Vajrayana traditions:

Approximately 490 million believers
TIBET: 1.6 million
TIBETANS & MONGOLS IN NORTHWESTERN CHINA: 14 million

MONGOLIA: 1.2 million
BHUTAN: 1.4 million
NEPAL: 6 million
CENTRAL ASIA: .3 million
CHINA: between 100 & 250 million
JAPAN: between 40 & 100 million
KOREA: approximately 20 million
TAIWAN: 6 million
SINGAPORE: 1 million
HONG KONG: 2 million
VIETNAM: 30 million

To which one must add minorities in Northern India, Indonesia, Malaysia, and Thailand.

3. Buddhism outside of Asia.

The number of Western Buddhists, including immigrants, cannot be established with certainty. One can estimate somewhere between 3 and 5 million for the United States, a half million for Canada, and about a million in Europe.

The lunar-solar calendar

Traditional societies in Asia follow a lunar or a lunar-solar calendar. It was only with the onset of Western influence at the end of the last century that most of them adopted the solar calendar. The lunar calendar, based on the lunar cycle, consists of months with 28 days, and requires intercalation to bring it into conformity with the solar calendar. The calendar varies from one country to another. In some places the New Year falls in February, in others in March.

Photo Credits

Sovraccoperta: Bruno Quaresima

Marco Bertona: 47a, 57, 88-89, 122

Bernard Faure: 53, 109b, 123b, 130s

Paola Ghirotti: 48b, 60, 91a, 92-93, 93, 94-95, 96-97, 97, 98a, 98b, 99, 102b, 103a, 110a, 112b, 113b, 117b, 119b, 121, 123a, 123c, 124, 125a, 128, 132bs, 132bd, 137b

Istituto Fotografico Editoriale SCALA: 10, 12, 13a, 14a, 14b, 15a, 16b, 19, 24, 26, 27, 28, 30, 37, 46, 64, 65, 103b, 105b, 112a, 126s, 131d, 135d

Marka: 2 (G. Simeone), 6 (Fototeca Storica Nazionale di Ando Gilardi), 8-9 (D. Cox), 13b (C. Pemberton, 15b (Fototeca Storica Nazionale di Ando Gilardi), 17a (A. Evrard), 17b (G. Tomsich), 20 (C. Mauri), 21 (Fototeca Storica Nazionale di Ando Gilardi), 22 (A. Evrard), 23 (Infinity), 25a (V. Pcholkin), 29 (Fototeca Storica Nazionale di Ando Gilardi), 30b e 31b (FPG), 31a , 32b (G. Hiller), 33 (Fototeca Storica Nazionale di Ando Gilardi), 34 (M. Cristofori), 35 (H. Kanus), 38a (J. Kugler), 38b (A. Tosatto), 39 (Infinity), 42 (Infinity), 43 (Fototeca Storica

Nazionale di Ando Gilardi), 44a (Fototeca Storica Nazionale di Ando Gilardi), 50 (D. Bartruff), 51 (M. Brooke), 54 (Impact Visual), 55 (Infinity), 56 (Infinity), 58 (C. Dogliani), 59 (D. Bartruff), 62-63 (D. Cox), 66-67 (C. Mauri), 68 (H. S. Huber), 69 (H.S. Huber), 70a, 70b (M. Monti), 71 (D. Ball), 72a (M. Cristofori), 72-73 (M. Cristofori), 74 (D. Ball), 75 (H. Kanus), 76-77 (Infinity), 78-79 (Infinity), 80 (E. Papetti), 81 a (E. Papetti), 81b (Vloo), 82-83 (Infinity), 83a (K. Su), 82c (Infinity), 82b (K. Su), 84-85 (Infinity), 86-87 (Infinity), 90a (A. Evrard), 90b (Infinity), 91b (Infinity), 105a (U. Isman), 106a (Infinity), 107 (Infinity), 108 (Fototeca Storica Nazionale di Ando Gilardi), 109a, 111 (R. Herzog), 114a (M. Brooke), 114b (H.S. Huber), 115 (H. Kanus), 116a (V. Pcholkin), 117a (Infinity), 119a (G. Tomsich), 126d (D. Cody), 128a (C. Silvestro), 129 (F. Giaccone), 132as (C. Pemberton), 133a (Photri), 133b (Infinity), 136as (R. Benzi), 136ac (R. Benzi), 136d (H. Kanus), 136bs (R. Benzi), 137a (FPG), 139

Virginio Nava: 36, 72b, 116b, 138

RCS Libri: 11